The Lost for Words Collection

Kathy Schmidt and Louise Jourdan

First published in 2014 by New Holland Publishers Pty Ltd
London • Sydney • Cape Town • Auckland

The Chandlery Unit 114 50 Westminster Bridge Road London SE1 7QY
1/66 Gibbes Street Chatswood NSW 2067 Australia
Wembley Square First Floor Solan Road Gardens Cape Town 8001 South Africa
218 Lake Road Northcote Auckland New Zealand

A record of this book is held at the British Library or the National Library of Australia.

ISBN 9781742574875

Publisher: Fiona Schultz
Editor: Liz Hardy
Designer: Keisha Galbraith
Production Manager: Olga Dementiev
Printer: Toppan Leefung Printing Ltd

10 9 8 7 6 5 4 3 2 1

Keep up with New Holland Publishers on Facebook
www.facebook.com/NewHollandPublishers

Contents

PREFACE

'All of us are walking around with some kind of birthday card we would like to give—some personal expression of joy, creativity or aliveness that we are hiding under our shirt.'
—Unknown

Have you ever bought a card for a friend or family member and been at a total loss for words? It is a familiar situation for all of us. We sit with our pen poised over the card for 20 minutes waiting for that lightning bolt of inspiration to flow through the pen and onto the card with something intelligent, amusing, caring or sympathetic. We want the receiver to be so moved by our words that they will want to keep it for eternity rather than discard it discreetly after a few days.

But in a last minute dash, and out of desperation, our masterpiece is more like:

To ....

Best wishes

From ....

It's a pretty poor effort, but we are not alone. Don't be afraid any longer of buying the perfect card that is blank inside. Let this book be your lifesaver and give you inspiration.

Birthday

*'Let us celebrate the occasion
with wine and sweet words.'*

— Plautus
(254—184 BC, Roman comic dramatist)

Today, on your birthday, I look back on all the times
I have been touched by your kindness.

✳

On your birthday, I want to thank you for making
such a beautiful difference in my life.

✳

I am so blessed that I have been part of your life for another year.

✳

Though we celebrate your birthday today, we have reason to celebrate
every day for having someone as wonderful as you in our lives.

✳

I hope you have a fantastic birthday. Thank you for being
such a wonderful friend and for all your support. I look
forward to many more years of friendship.

✳

With love on your special day.

✳

I hope you have a great birthday filled with many surprises.

✳

I hope it will be a special and memorable day.

✳

Happy birthday to my disco diva.

✳

May your birthday be everything beautiful,
everything special, everything happy.

✳

Have a happy day, celebrating with family and friends
and reminiscing about birthdays gone by.

✳

May happiness be in your heart on your birthday and always.

It's your [age] birthday. I wish you many more
birthdays to come.

*

We hope you really enjoyed your [age] birthday and
we are glad we could celebrate it with you.

*

Happy [age] birthday. Things keep getting better and better.

*

You have achieved so much in your first [age] years and
I am looking forward to what is yet to come.

*

On your birthday, I want you to know how blessed
I am to have you in my life.

*

Don't think of yourself as going to seed ... think of yourself
as being ready to blossom! Happy birthday.

*

On your birthday, some words of wisdom: smile
while you still have teeth! Happy birthday.

*

To my dear friend, who was born in the days when things
were made to last, you don't look a day over [age].

*

You know you're getting older when your knees
buckle and your belt won't. Happy birthday.

*

Don't do anything embarrassing on your birthday this year.
You don't have as much time to live it down as you used to.

*

I realise that getting old can seem intimidating at first.
But what's it like now? Happy birthday.

Honey, I knew you'd appreciate a relaxing, home-cooked
meal for your birthday. So I called your mother and
she said Wednesday was fine.

✳

Don't worry, sister, you're not getting older ... just more like mum.

✳

As we grow older, we often find that it is better to light one small
candle than to be seen in fluorescent lighting. Happy birthday.

✳

You know you're getting older when your children
begin to look middle-aged.

✳

You're not getting a year older. You're getting another
year to shop! Happy birthday.

✳

You deserve to be spoilt rotten on your birthday.

✳

May all your dreams come true in this special birthday year.

✳

Hoping your birthday brings with it all the things your heart holds
dear.

✳

We all agree you're looking younger than ever ... Happy Birthday.

✳

It's your day—so relax and enjoy all the good things coming your way.

✳

May your Happy Birthday be perfect.

✳

What a special day, the day you came into the world.
My life has been all the better for knowing you.

How would I describe (name)? In a word ... seasoned.

✳

May all the wishes you make today come true.

✳

When I see beauty, I think of you ... Happy Birthday.

✳

No-one can avoid the passing of time, so smile and enjoy every minute.

✳

You're only as old as you feel ... Happy Birthday.

✳

Fabulous, flirty and (age) ... Happy Birthday.

✳

Wishing you love, joy and laughter on your day.

✳

May your birthday be as warm and beautiful to you as you are to me.

✳

May your day be so happy that your face hurts from smiling.

✳

On your birthday, I just want to acknowledge the joy you bring to all those around you.

✳

Wish for the stars ... you deserve it.

✳

May all life's simple pleasures be yours today.

✳

Do you feel a little wiser? Happy Birthday.

As the years go by we all soften a little around the edges.

✱

Embrace life and all it holds for you.

✱

May this year hold many fond memories for the future.

✱

To my dear friend who lights up the room.

✱

On the endless possibilities for the coming year ... dream big.

✱

You make all the difference in my life.

✱

No-one deserves a special day as much as you.

✱

We take pleasure in celebrating your birthday as it is a reminder of how lucky we are to have you in our life. You are a wonderful (brother/sister/daughter/friend etc).

✱

You will never go out of style.

✱

To the star of the show ... Happy Birthday.
A year older and getting better with age.

✱

Another year of life, another year of experience. May you continue to age with wisdom.

✱

You did it... you completed another lap around the sun! Congratulations.

Make a wish for every candle on your cake. You deserve all the happiness in the world.

*

To my friend who never seems to age... Happy Birthday.

*

Like a bottle of fine wine, each year you are better than the one before.

*

You are too marvellous for words... Happy Birthday.

*

Today you are a year older, but you will be forever awesome.

*

It's just a number... Happy Birthday!

*

It's your special day, but you are special every day!

*

It's a day to celebrate! Another year with you in my life.

*

Although I am not there to celebrate with you, I send you a beautiful bouquet of birthday wishes.

*

You will always be younger than... tomorrow! Happy Birthday.

*

The survey results are in. This birthday and the year ahead are going to be your best ones yet!

*

Every day is a new beginning, but a birthday is the celebration of a special new beginning.

Wishing you a day that is as special as you are to me.

*

It's a day to celebrate all you have achieved and for me/us to celebrate having you in my/our lives.

*

Dear Brother/Sister, Today I am celebrating that someone even more annoying than you wasn't born into this family.
Just kidding. Happy Birthday.

*

I hope you enjoy your birthday as much as I enjoy having you as my friend.

*

To my forever-young friend, wishing you many more years of health and prosperity.

*

Although you are another year older, you will never
go out of style.

*

I will never take having you in my life for granted. Today is your birthday and I want you to know just how special you are, and how much you mean to me.

*

Happy Birthday [name], I just wanted to let you know that I appreciate you, and I know how hard it is to find a friend as wonderful as you.

*

*Birthdays are good for you. The more you have,
the longer you live.* Unknown

✳

'Our birthdays are feathers in the broad wing of time.'
Johann Friedrich Richter (1763–1825), German author

✳

*'Birthdays? yes, in a general way;
For the most if not for the best of men:
You were born (I suppose) on a certain day:
So was I: or perhaps in the night: what then?'*
James Kenneth Stephen (1859–92), British poet

✳

*'From our birthday, until we die,
Is but the winking of an eye.'*
William Butler Yeats (1865–1939), Irish poet

✳

*'There are three hundred and sixty-four days when
you might get un-birthday presents ... and only one
for birthday presents, you know.'*
Lewis Carroll (1832–98), British writer and mathematician

✳

*'Old age: A great sense of calm and freedom. When the
passions have relaxed their hold, you may have escaped,
not from one master but from many.'*
Plato (427–347 BC), Greek philosopher

✳

*'... the birthday of my life
Is come, my love is come to me.'*
Christina Georgina Rossetti (1830–94), British poet

'One of the signs of passing youth is the birth of a sense of fellowship with other human beings as we take our place among them.'
Virginia Woolf (1882–1941), British novelist

*

'The greatest comfort of my old age, and that which gives me the highest satisfaction, is the pleasing remembrance of the many benefits and friendly offices I have done to others.'
Marcus Cato (95-46BC), Roman statesman,
soldier and Stoic philosopher

*

'May you live all the days of your life.'
Jonathan Swift (1667–1745), British satirical writer,
born in Ireland

*

'Grow old along with me! The best is yet to be, the last of life, for which the first was made.'
Robert Browning (1812–89), British poet

*

The best birthdays of all are those that haven't arrived yet.
Robert Orben

*

Wisdom doesn't necessarily come with age. Sometimes age just shows up all by itself. Tom Wilson

*

The old believe everything; the middle-aged suspect everything; the young know everything. Oscar Wilde

*

When I was younger, I could remember anything, whether it happened or not. Mark Twain

*

Few women admit their age. Few men act theirs. Unknown

Time may be a great healer, but it's a lousy beautician.
Unknown

✳

What could be more beautiful than a dear old lady growing wise with age? Every age can be enchanting, provided you live within it.
Brigitte Bardot

The older I grow the more I distrust the familiar doctrine that age brings wisdom. H J Mencken

✳

Count your life by smiles, not tears. Count your age by friends, not years. Unknown

The secret of staying young is to live honestly, eat slowly, and lie about your age. Lucille Ball

✳

The best way to remember your wife's birthday is to forget it once.
H V Prochnow

✳

I never forget my wife's birthday. It's usually the day after she reminds me about it. Unknown

✳

A well adjusted woman is one who not only knows what she wants for her birthday, but even knows what she's going to exchange it for. Unknown

✳

You were born an original. Don't die a copy. John Mason

✳

The more you praise and celebrate your life, the more there is in life to celebrate. Oprah Winfrey

✳

Age is not measured by years. Nature does not equally distribute energy. Some people are born old and tired while others are going strong at seventy. Dorothy Thompson

✳

At twenty years of age, the will reigns; at thirty, the wit; and at forty, the judgement. Benjamin Franklin

✳

From birth to age eighteen, a girl needs good parents. From eighteen to thirty-five, she needs good looks. From thirty-five to fifty-five, she needs a good personality. From fifty-five on, she needs good cash. Sophie Tucker

✳

And in the end, it's not the years in your life that count. It's the life in your years. Abraham Lincoln

✳

Age is strictly a case of mind over matter. If you don't mind, it doesn't matter. Jack Benny

✳

It is better to wear out than to rust out.
Bishop Richard Cumberland

FUNNY BIRTHDAY QUOTES

'Inside every older person is a younger person wondering what the hell happened.'
Cora Harvey Armstrong, US gospel singer

✳

'To me, old age is always fifteen years older than I am.'
Bernard Mannes Baruch (1870–1965),
US politician and financier

✳

'Of late I appear
To have reached that stage
When people look old
Who are only my age.'
Richard Armour (1906–89), US poet and humorist

'A diplomat is a man who always remembers a
woman's birthday but never remembers her age.'
Robert Frost (1874–1963), US poet

*

'You are only young once, but you can be immature for a lifetime.'
John P. Grier, unknown

*

'If I'd known I was going to live this long,
I'd have taken better care of myself.'
Eubie Blake (1883–1983), US musician, on his 100th birthday

*

'Men are like wine. Some turn to vinegar,
but the best improve with age.'
C.E.M. Joad (1891–1953), British broadcaster and philosopher

*

'Let us respect grey hairs, especially our own.' J.P. Sears, unknown

*

'Age is a high price to pay for maturity.'
Tom Stoppard (born 1937), British playwright,
born in Czechoslovakia

*

'If we could be twice young and twice old
we could correct all our mistakes.'
Euripides (480–406? BC), Athenian tragician

*

'Growing old is like being increasingly
penalised for a crime you have not committed.'
—Anthony Dymoke Powell (1905–2000), British author

Belated Birthday

I heard it was your birthday... you don't look any older;
no wonder I missed it.

✳

I missed your birthday... You can't blame me, you have had so many
I lost track of time.

✳

Happy early birthday for next year!

✳

I thought we rescheduled? No? Happy Belated Birthday.

✳

You can't be [age]. Someone must have stopped the clock!

✳

I am so excited to be celebrating [age] years of [name]. It has been
wonderful to be with you and watch you grow and change.

✳

You're so HOT... If you were any hotter you would be me.
Happy Birthday.

✳

You know me... Always fashionably late. Happy Birthday.

✳

Just helping to prolong the celebration. Happy Belated Birthday.

✳

Oh well, at least I remembered that I forgot ... Happy Belated Birthday

✳

You may think this card is late
But you'll have to change your tune...
It's not [4] days too late
But [361] days too soon.

How do you expect me to remember your birthday, when you never look any older?

Child's Birthday

Have a great birthday and eat lots of cake.

✳

May your birthday be a happy day with lots of fun and may it bring all the things that birthday girls/boys love.

✳

Have a wonderful day you gorgeous girl/beautiful boy.
To my lovely (granddaughter/son, little friend, niece/nephew).
I love you very much. Have a wonderful birthday.

✳

May all your birthday wishes come true.
Have a wonderful day and enjoy your present.

✳

Have a super, wonderful, fabulous, fantastic, totally cool birthday. May you be spoiled rotten!

✳

Wishing you a special day when everything goes your way.

✳

[Number] candles on a cake ... Have a great day.

✳

A special day with gifts and friends. You deserve this and so much more.

✳

Hoping every day is full of new adventures. Have fun being [age].

We hope you enjoy your [age] birthday and all your
pressies, cake, lollies and all the other stuff involved
with these things called 'birthdays'.

✳

Happy Birthday—you're [age]. We hope you have fun
with your family and all your friends.

✳

We hope you have lots of fun and get loads of pressies.

✳

Lots of laughs and lots of fun on the happiest
day of the year, your birthday.

✳

A lifetime of joy and happiness to you.

Turning Ten

Double figures – Wow!
Who's a big (boy/girl) now?

✳

Happy Birthday, ten-year-old ... you hardly look a day over nine.

✳

Hooray! You're turning 10 today.

✳

Congratulations. Ten years old ... and ten years wiser.

✳

Turning 10. Congratulations on reaching double figures.

✳

Happy Birthday to an amazing 10-year-old who's smart and clever
with so much to offer. Keep learning and living every day.

Wishing you a birthday as awesome as you are. Happy 10th Birthday.

✳

Wow! Ten years old ... a little bit taller than last year ... does that mean more cake for you and less for me?

✳

Wow! 10 years old ... getting closer to 100 every day!

✳

To a little ray of sunshine, shining brighter each year ... 10 today ... Hooray!

✳

10 today ... now the adventure begins.

✳

Candy is sweet but you are sweeter! Happy Birthday 10-year-old.

✳

Happy three thousand seven hundred and sixty eighth day!

✳

Happy Birthday 10-year-old. You only look a day over 9.

✳

Unless you want to end up old and wrinkled, it's best to stop having birthdays.

✳

Go bananas ... it's your 10th birthday

✳

Only 112 years and 164 more days until you can be in the *Guinness Book of World Records*.

✳

10! You're getting old now. Have you found any grey hairs yet?

Thirteen

It's an age of change. Don't worry, your parents are just as frightened as you are. Happy Birthday.

✳

Hey 13-year-old, getting old now ... it won't be long till you retire.

✳

Youth comes but once in a lifetime—don't grow up too fast. Have a great day.

✳

Oh, the teenage years ... I am so excited for you! And so afraid for your parents.

✳

Remember ... now that you're a teen, you shouldn't do anything that wouldn't make your mother proud.

✳

Thirteen. Now, that's a reason to be excited. It's the beginning of an amazing time of your life.

✳

So now you're 13 ... what does that mean? Making fun of 12-year-olds, perhaps?

✳

It's your 13th birthday. May 13 wishes come true for you today.

Funky and fabulous ... you must be fourteen. Oops, that's next year ... Happy Birthday.

✳

A 13th birthday is an event not to be missed ... thank you for sharing your company on this special day.

✳

It's your 13th birthday ... relax, chill out and enjoy the ride.

Now you are 13 you will face new challenges ... be true to yourself
and stay strong in your beliefs and you will surely succeed in
everything you do.

✳

The 13th birthday is such a special milestone ... cherish each
moment and all you have achieved so far.

✳

It's a milestone year with big changes ahead... try not to cause your
parents too much worry.

✳

You're now a teenager. Take it slow and make sure you enjoy these
special years.

✳

WOW, 13 today. These are the years where you gain some
independence. Make sure you take the time to think about your
actions, so that these are the best years of your life.

✳

Enjoy your teens... more independence without major responsibilities.
Make the most of it!

✳

Happy Birthday to the coolest teenager I know. Wishing you a wicked
day and an awesome future.

Girl Sixteen

Sweet 16 and never been kissed ... or so you tell your parents.

✳

Sixteen is a magical time ... Enjoy every moment ... Happy 16th.

You turn 16 on this day, and I'm pleased to say,
with sweetness still intact.

*

Happy Birthday to a girl who has grown into a level-headed young
woman. Your maturity and confidence at 16 have impressed us.

*

When you came into our lives 16 years ago, we were so blessed. May
you continue to bring joy to those around you. Happy Birthday.

*

You're finally turning 16. What a great time to celebrate.

*

Enjoy being 16. It's that glorious time of feeling grown up but without
the burden of big responsibilities.

*

Happy Birthday to the sweet 16. So young and beautiful, nothing
compares to how special you are.

*

Beautiful 16-year-old, be strong in yourself and let your beauty shine
from within.

*

To a true beauty ... Happy Sweet 16th.

*

Happy 16th Birthday ... may every day be a good hair day.

*

To my style queen ... happy 16th.

*

To a special 16-year-old, whatever dreams you hold, may the future
bring them to you.

The love of family and friends will be with you today (and maybe a few secret admirers as well). Enjoy your special day.

✱

May this day be as special as you are. Never think of yourself as anything less than priceless.

✱

To the sweetest 16-year-old I know, wishing you a wonderful year of new discoveries.

✱

A 16th birthday is another step closer to adulthood. You can now learn to drive and really cause your parents to tear their hair out!

✱

To an innocent and sweet 16. I am sure butter wouldn't melt in your mouth.

✱

Always act like you're wearing an invisible crown,
I do. Unknown

✱

Say goodbye to dolls and toys. Say hello to make-up and boys!
Unknown

Boy Sixteen

Happy 16th ... Not long till that motorbike license ... Parents beware!

✱

To a 16-year-old legend ... Happy Birthday.

✱

Just remember ... 16, not 18. Take it easy and enjoy your day.

✱

Happy 16th. Enjoy the year ... one of the best of your life.

No need to drive pretend cars on video games any more, now you are old enough to experience the real thing.

✳

To a wonderful 16-year-old who makes a wonderful role model to those around him. Congratulations on this milestone birthday.

✳

It's been wonderful to watch you grow and mature over the years. Not long until adulthood, but make sure you take the time to enjoy these growing years.

✳

You have been taller than me for a few years now but I am still your mother. Happy 16th Birthday.

✳

Off to the motor registry to get your learner's permit. If you need someone to take you for lessons I am busy that day.
Happy 16th Birthday

✳

Sweet sixteen! Sweet sixteen!
We can't believe it's true;
The person sitting before us
Is really, really you.

Sweet sixteen! Sweet sixteen!
Coloured candles on a cake!
We send you a Happy Birthday
With a wish for you to make!
Shirley J. Davidson

✳

Reaching 16 is a milestone,
a happy point in life.
You've set your personality.
and your tolerance for strife.

By now you know right from wrong
and how to influence friends.

It's time to look down the road
at forks and around the bends.

The road ahead is wonderful,
some choices will be clear.
Your path depends on bravery
to push aside the fear.

When you chose this way or that,
slow choices or if snappy,
make the choices best for you,
the ones that make you happy.
Unknown

Eighteen

18? Congratulations! Now you can finally say
'Stop treating me like a kid'.

✳

Now that you're 18 society feels you are mature enough to vote.
The first thing to vote for is an all-night party to celebrate.

✳

Now that you're 18 freedom is yours ... what are you waiting for?
Happy Birthday.

✳

Turning 18, what does that really mean? It means you can vote, drink
and be tried as an adult in court. What, not as exciting
as you thought?! Have a great day.

✳

You're not just 18 today—you're all the ages you've ever been.
So now that you're an adult, don't forget the kid inside.

✳

Now that you're 18 the world is your oyster ... what's first
on the agenda?

Registering to vote?
Joining the army?
Moving out of home?
Or just having a massive party? ... Happy Birthday

✳

Happy 18th birthday. May this year, your first officially
as an adult, be simply amazing.

✳

Now you are legally allowed to do all those things you have been
doing since you [or I] were [or was] 14.

✳

This birthday marks the beginning of adulthood. Doesn't mean you
can't still be a child at heart!

✳

Welcome to the next stage of your life. Up until now your childish
charm got you by... now you will need to rely on your good looks.

✳

Turning 18 means there are new and amazing opportunities ahead. I
have no doubt you will take it all in your stride.

✳

It has been wonderful to watch you transition from child to teenager
and now an adult. I have no doubt that your future is bright and you
will achieve everything you set your mind to.

✳

Common sense is the collection of prejudices acquired by age 18.
Albert Einstein

✳

*I cried on my 18th birthday. I thought 17 was such a nice age.
You're young enough to get away with things,
but you're old enough, too.* Liv Tyler

Twenty-one

21 ... Congratulations—the beginning of a new phase in your life. Make it an exciting one.

✱

You make this world a better place, you deserve this special day. Lots of love on your 21st birthday.

✱

Happy 21st. Looking forward to watching all your dreams come true.

✱

At 21, you feel like you can take on the world. Have fun trying.

✱

Congratulations on turning 21. May doors open to new and wonderful opportunities.

✱

There is a special name for people who stay home on their birthday ... LOSER ... Hope you have a great night out on your 21st birthday.

✱

Happy 21st birthday ... this is just the start of amazing things to come.

✱

Here's to you on your 21st birthday. Have a good one!

✱

May this day be as warm and wonderful as you are ... Happy 21st.

✱

So now you are 21 ... growing up is still optional! Happy Birthday.

✱

We are so happy to be able to celebrate this special day and all the achievements you have made along the way ... Happy 21st!

Sending you the priceless wishes of love, strength, courage and wisdom on this milestone birthday

✳

A milestone year! Make sure you take the time to stop and reflect on all you have achieved.

✳

Your 21st birthday is much like New Year's Eve: a time to set new goals and plans for the future. All the best for everything you set out to achieve.

✳

To the most well adjusted 21-year-old I know. It has been such a pleasure watching you grow up into an amazing adult. You are truly a role model to those around you.

✳

This is the beginning of your adult years, but never lose that childish charm that makes you so endearing to everyone you meet.

for Teens/The Young

One of the advantages of being young is that you don't let common sense get in the way of doing things everyone else knows are impossible. Unknown

✳

Today, be aware of how you are spending your 1440 beautiful moments, and spend them wisely. Unknown

✳

No man is ever old enough to know better. Holbrook Jackson

✳

The longer I live the more beautiful life becomes.
Frank Lloyd Wright

The surprising thing about young fools is how many survive to become old fools. Doug Larson

✻

Unless you try to do something beyond what you have already mastered, you will never grow. Ronald E Osborn

✻

Start by doing what's necessary; then do what's possible; and suddenly you are doing the impossible. St Francis of Assisi

✻

Remember, if you ever need a helping hand, you'll find one at the end of your arm ... As you grow older you will discover that you have two hands. One for helping yourself, the other for helping others. Audrey Hepburn

✻

Success does not come to those who wait ... and it does not wait for anyone to come to it. Unknown

✻

Start where you are. Distant fields always look greener, but opportunity lies right where you are. Take advantage of every opportunity of service. Robert Collier

✻

Start every day with an inspiring thought. Unknown

✻

The real secret of success is enthusiasm. Walter Chrysler

✻

Remember that as a teenager you are in the last stage of your life when you will be happy to hear the phone is for you. Fran Leibowitz

✻

The best way to keep children at home is to make the home atmosphere pleasant, and let the air out of the tyres.
Dorothy Parker

You can only be young once. But you can always be immature.
Dave Barry

✱

When buying a used car, punch the buttons on the radio. If all the stations are rock and roll, there's a good chance the transmission is shot. Larry Lujack

✱

The invention of the teenager was a mistake. Once you identify a period of life in which people get to stay out late but don't have to pay taxes—naturally, no-one wants to live any other way.
Judith Martin

✱

Mothers of teenagers know why animals eat their young.
Unknown

30th and 35th Birthday Quotes

When you turn 30, a whole new thing happens: you see yourself acting like your parents. Blair Sabol

✱

After 30, a body has a mind of its own. Bette Midler

✱

A man 30 years old, I said to myself, should have his field of life all ploughed, and his planting well done; for after that it is summer time. Lew Wallace

✱

'Everything I know I learned after I was thirty.'
—Georges Clemenceau (1841–1929), French politician

✱

'Time and Tide wait for no man, but time always stands still for a woman of thirty.'
—Robert Frost (1874–1963), US poet

*'Thirty-five is when you finally get your head together
and your body starts falling apart.'*
—Caryn Leschen, US graphic artist

✳

*'Thirty-five is a very attractive age; London society
is full of women who have of their own free choice
remained thirty-five for years.'*
—Oscar Wilde (1854—1900), Irish dramatist and novelist

40th Birthday Quotes

'Life begins at forty.'
—W.B. Pitkin (1878—1953), US writer

✳

Be wise with speed; a fool at 40 is a fool indeed.
Edward Young

✳

Every man over 40 is a scoundrel. George Bernard Shaw

✳

You're not 40, you're 18 with 22 years' experience. Unknown

✳

*What most persons consider as virtue after the age of 40
is simply a loss of energy.* Voltaire

✳

*The best years of a woman's life—the ten years between 39 and
40.* Unknown

✳

*Life begins at 40—but so do fallen arches, rheumatism, faulty
eyesight, and the tendency to tell a story to the same person,
three or four times.* Helen Rowland

At the age of 20, we don't care what the world thinks of us; at 30, we worry about what it is thinking of us; at 40, we discover that it wasn't thinking of us at all. Unknown

✳

The 'I just woke up' face of your thirties is the 'all day long' face of your forties. Libby Reid

✳

When I passed forty I dropped pretense, 'cause men like women who got some sense. Maya Angelou

OLDER Birthday Quotes

'The years between fifty and seventy are the hardest. You are always being asked to do things, and yet you are not decrepit enough to turn them down.' —TS Eliot (1888—1965), British poet

✳

Looking 50 is great—if you're 60. Joan Rivers

✳

The man who views the world at 50 the same as he did at 20 has wasted 30 years of his life. Muhammad Ali

✳

I think when the full horror of being 50 hits you, you should stay home and have a good cry. Alan Bleasdale

✳

Forty is the old age of youth; 50 is the youth of old age. Unknown

✳

I'm aiming by the time I'm 50 to stop being an adolescent. Wendy Cope

✳

Nature gives you the face you have at twenty, but it's up to you to merit the face you have at fifty. Coco Chanel

*'A man of sixty has spent twenty years in bed
and over three years in eating.'*
Arnold Bennett (1867–1931), English novelist

✳

Some people reach the age of 60 before others. Lord Hood

✳

*I have achieved my 70 years in the usual way, by sticking strictly to a
scheme of life which would kill anybody else ... I will offer here, as a
sound maxim, this: That we can't reach old age by another man's road.*
Mark Twain, at his 70th birthday dinner

✳

One starts to get young at the age of 60 and then it is too late.
Pablo Picasso

✳

*If I had to live again I would do exactly the same thing. Of course I
have regrets, but if you are 60 years old and you have
no regrets then you haven't lived.* Christy Moore

✳

Oh to be 70 again.
Georges Clemenceau

✳

*Age is not measured by years. Nature does not equally distribute
energy. Some people are born old and tired while others
are going strong at 70.* Dorothy Thompson

✳

*By the time you're 80 years old you've learned everything.
You only have to remember it.* George Burns

✳

*A man of 80 has outlived probably three new schools of painting,
two of architecture and poetry and a hundred in dress.*
Joyce Carey

The advantage of being eighty years old is that one has many people to love. Jean Renoir

Middle Age Quotes

'Middle age: When you begin to exchange your emotions for symptoms.'
Georges Clemenceau (1841–1929), French politician

✳

'Middle age occurs when you are too young to take up golf and too old to rush up to the net.'
Franklin Pierce Adams (1881–1960), US columnist

✳

Middle age is when a guy keeps turning off lights for economical rather than romantic reasons. Eli Cass

✳

Middle age is when work is a lot less fun and fun is a lot more work. Unknown

✳

Middle age is when your age starts to show around your middle. Bob Hope

✳

Probably the happiest period in life most frequently is in middle age, when the eager passions of youth are cooled, and the infirmities of age not yet begun; as we see that the shadows, which are at morning and evening so large, almost entirely disappear at midday. Thomas Arnold

✳

The only time you really live fully is from 30 to 60. The young are slaves to dreams; the old servants of regrets. Only the middle-aged have all their five senses in the keeping of their wits. Hervey Allen

Middle age is the awkward period when Father Time catches up with Mother Nature. Harold Coffin

✳

The really frightening thing about middle age is that you know you'll grow out of it. Doris Day

✳

At middle age the soul should be opening up like a rose, not closing up like a cabbage. John Andrew Holmes

✳

Middle age is when you've met so many people that every new person you meet reminds you of someone else. Ogden Nash

Old Age Quotes

'Nobody loves life like him that's growing old'
Sophocles (495–406? BC), Greek tragedian

✳

'The greatest problem about old age is the fear that it may go on too long.'
A.J.P. Taylor (1906–90), British historian

✳

'Old age is the most unexpected of all things that happens to a man.'
Leon Trotsky (1879–1940), Russian revolutionary leader

✳

'Don't look back. Something might be gaining on you.'
Satchel Paige (1906–82), US baseball pitcher

✳

'Old age isn't so bad when you consider the alternative.'
Maurice Chevalier (1888–1972), French actor and singer

'Youth is a blunder; manhood a struggle; old age a regret.'
—Benjamin Disraeli (1804—81), British politician and novelist

✻

We know we're getting old when the only thing we want for our birthday is not to be reminded of it. Unknown

✻

I still have a full deck; I just shuffle slower now. Unknown

✻

Old age is like everything else. To make a success of it, you've got to start young. Fred Astaire

✻

Therefore we do not lose heart. Even though our outward man is perishing, yet the inward man is being renewed day by day.
The Bible, 2 Corinthians 4:16

✻

To resist the frigidity of old age, one must combine the body, the mind, and the heart. And to keep these in parallel vigour one must exercise, study, and love. Bonstettin

✻

By the time you find greener pastures, you can't climb the fence!
Unknown

✻

You don't stop laughing because you grow old. You grow old because you stop laughing. Michael Pritchard

✻

Growing old is inevitable ... growing up is optional. Unknown

✻

You are never too old to set another goal or to dream a new dream. Les Brown

To keep the heart unwrinkled, to be hopeful, kindly, cheerful, reverent, that is to triumph over old age. Thomas B Aldrich

✻

I'm at an age when my back goes out more than I do. Phyllis Diller

✻

You're never too old to become younger. Mae West

✻

Just remember, once you're over the hill you begin to pick up speed. Charles Schulz

✻

In case you're worried about what is going to become of the younger generation, it's going to grow up and start worrying about the younger generation. Roger Allen

✻

Youth is a circumstance you can't do anything about. The trick is to grow up without getting old. Frank Lloyd Wright

✻

It is not all bad, this getting old, ripening. After the fruit has got its growth it should juice up and mellow. God forbid I should live long enough to ferment and rot and fall to the ground in a squash. Emily Carr

✻

Age is a high price to pay for maturity. Tom Stoppard

✻

They say that age is all in your mind. The trick is keeping it from creeping down into your body. Unknown

✻

Growing old is like being increasing penalised for a crime you have not committed. Anthony Powell

Lying about my age is easier now, since I sometimes forget what it is. Unknown

✳

No wise man ever wished to be younger. Jonathan Swift

✳

In youth we run into difficulties. In old age difficulties run into us. Josh Billings

✳

You know you are getting old when the candles cost more than the cake. Bob Hope

✳

I'm very pleased with each advancing year. It stems back to when I was 40. I was a bit upset about reaching that milestone, but an older friend consoled me. 'Don't complain about growing old—many, many people do not have that privilege.' Earl Warren

✳

Wisdom doesn't automatically come with old age. Nothing does—except wrinkles. It's true, some wines improve with age. But only if the grapes were good in the first place. Abigail Van Buren

✳

It's hard to be nostalgic when you can't remember anything! Unknown

✳

It's sad to grow old, but nice to ripen. Brigitte Bardot

✳

The older the fiddler, the sweeter the tune. English Proverb

✳

Old age: A great sense of calm and freedom. When the passions have relaxed their hold, you may have escaped, not from one master but from many. Plato

Youth is happy because it has the ability to see beauty. Anyone who keeps the ability to see beauty never grows old. Franz Kafka

✳

Some people, no matter how old they get, never lose their beauty—they merely move it from their faces into their hearts.
Martin Buxbaum

✳

Old age is no place for sissies. Bette Davis

✳

By the time you find greener pastures, you can't climb the fence!
Unknown

valentines

'For, you see, each day I love you more,
today more than yesterday
and less than tomorrow.'
—Rosemonde Gerard (1871–1953),
US writer

I think I have found my friend for life.

✳

My heart skips a beat every time I think of you and the
times we have shared. I'll never let you go.

✳

I really want you to know you're my special someone ...
a cool breeze on a hot day.

✳

You're the only one for me. I long for a place in your
heart. When I see your face I know the future is bright.

✳

My first thoughts of the day are always of you.

✳

For you there is nothing I would not do, as your
love is etched upon my heart.

✳

To my beautiful wife/girlfriend who is always spending
her love with kind and thoughtful gestures.

✳

You are like a beautiful diamond, admired and precious.

✳

You have touched my heart in a way no-one else has or ever could.
You're the fire in my heart. I'll love you always.

✳

My eyes are drawn to your breath-taking beauty.

✳

To the woman who captured my love and admiration.

✳

Thinking of you brings such warmth to my heart ...
no-one can compare to you or the love we share.

Words cannot describe the overwhelming feelings of love and passion I have for you.

✳

You transport me to paradise. You transform my dreams and aspirations.
I did not know that such love could exist till I met you.

✳

I want to hold you close, care for you, protect you and love you always.

✳

The love I have within my heart will last forever.

✳

In my heart I keep the sparkle of your eyes and your warm smile.

✳

To my warm, vibrant and intelligent girlfriend/boyfriend/ husband/wife. You grow more special to me every day.

✳

Even though we may be apart, you are always with me.
I would send you a kiss but the postman might steal it.

✳

I just wanted to say, I think you're special every day.

✳

Sweetpea, you have stolen my heart.

✳

You make me the man/woman I am. I give you my heart.

✳

My deepest thoughts are always of you.

✳

If you will just be mine, we will never part.

Let me give you my arms so I can hold you forever.

✱

I would walk a thousand miles just to spend
all my days with you by my side.

✱

When I think of love I think of you and your radiant smile.

✱

It has been said it is impossible to love and be wise.
But for you I can't help but to love.

✱

I once heard love ceases to be a pleasure when it ceases to be
a secret. Happy Valentine's Day, love your secret admirer.

✱

May our hearts touch softly on this special day.

✱

Beautiful girl ... I will love you forever.

✱

I am so happy you came into my life with all your beautiful qualities.

✱

With you in my life, I awake each day happy.

✱

I will always be yours and you will always be mine.
The most beautiful view is the one I share with you. Unknown

✱

You are the only one I wish to spend this day with.
Thank you for being my Valentine.

✱

You caught my eye, then captured my heart.

To me you are love personified. I hear love in your voice,
see love in your eyes and feel love in your touch.
Thank you for the beauty of your love each day.

✻

I have never known a love so strong, so secure; a place for us
to dwell side by side from here to eternity.

✻

To my Valentine, I need to take this moment to let you know how
much I value our love and how much it means to have you in my life.
Words cannot express the happiness you bring into my life each day.

✻

To the sweetest thing in the world ... I love you sweetie pie.

✻

I long to call you mine, sweet Valentine.

✻

I have not been feeling myself lately. I am weak at the knees, my brain
is like mush, I cannot sleep at night, my heart is racing and my
stomach is doing flips and it's all because of you
and the wonderful way you make me feel inside.

✻

To the love of my life—may your day be filled with love, laughter
and smiles. Love and kisses ...

✻

I love the words you say, the things you do and the way you show the
love we share in our lives each day.

✻

Two hearts beating together no matter how adverse the weather.

✻

The love in your smile makes me feel that all is possible. I love you.

✻

You catch me when I fall and pick me up when I am down.

Although we are apart and the days are so long, I will never stop counting the days till we can be together and at last forever.

*

From the moment we met our spirits united, from the moment we met my heart was in love with you. From the moment we met I wanted to share my life with you. I love you.

*

If we had never met, where would I be? Searching the world far and wide till I had you by my side.

*

When the sun has set and the day is done, come home to me and let's have some fun!

*

Your love shines so bright in my life that it makes all my woes disappear.

*

Love isn't always easy, but you're worth it. I'll love you always.

*

'You and me' is everything to me ... It's all I dream to ever be ... Thanks for the love you give to me.

*

I've been thinking of you today.

*

When I feel life gets too hard and I feel broken inside, you have always been the only one who could put me back together.

*

It took so long for us to find each other. So long for you to walk into my life. Now that you are here, I will hold onto you forever. I need you in my life.

All I have I give to you ... this is me, my heart, my love,
I give it all to you. I love you.

✻

Our lives together have been a wonderful adventure. Ups and downs,
twists and turns. I wouldn't have it any other way.

✻

Thank you for believing in me and my hopes and dreams for the future.
Please be with me every step of the way.

✻

Across the miles I send you smiles and
on the wings of a dove I send you love.

✻

I believe in you and the love we share. I believe it will
last a lifetime through the good times and the hard times.
I believe we can stand the test of time.

✻

My heart chose you, and I wouldn't have it any other way.

✻

As the stars in the sky, the sand on the beach, the drops
in the ocean are endless, so is this love of ours.

✻

When I hear music ... I think of you
When I hear laughter ... I think of you
When I feel warmth ... I think of you ...
because you are the most beautiful thing in my life.

✻

It is a miracle that we found each other. A gift from God ...
from me to you and you to me.

✻

I feel blessed as blessed can be ... simply because you want me.

You make me feel like sunshine.

✳

Somebody loves you ... somebody needs you ... all my love
from the bottom of my heart.

✳

What would I do without you? 'Cause love is me and you.

✳

Even when we are not together, you are always with me,
safe in the love that encompasses us.

✳

Even though we are far apart, our love stretches from heart to heart.

✳

I store the memories of the love we share deep in my heart
and seal it with a kiss.

You make me so mad... mad with love.

✳

I love you more than I love wearing my pyjamas all day long.

✳

When I fell for you I fell forever.

✳

When I met you, I was like a jigsaw that just found the missing piece.

✳

I fell so far and I could never go back.

✳

Just the thought of you makes me gooey inside.

✳

When you hold me I feel as though I will never be lost in this world again.

Some people mean more than words or emotions can express. [name] know that you are so precious and mean the world to me.

✳

Every day is brighter because of you.
Thank you for the faith you have in us... I love you.

✳

I love you because you make every day sunny and warm.

✳

All I want this day is to feel your embrace.

✳

When you touched my heart it drove me crazy... I cannot live another day without you.

✳

Our love is like a circle: it never ends.
Our love is like a raging river that cannot be tamed.

✳

I have never known a love as deep as this.

Valentine Quotes

'Life has taught us that love does not consist in gazing at each other but in looking outward together in the same direction.'
Antoine de Saint-Exupéry (1900–44), French pilot and poet

✳

'I arise from dreams of thee
In the first sweet sleep of night,
When the winds are breathing low,
And the stars are shining bright.'
Percy Bysshe Shelley (1792–1822), British poet

✳

Gravitation is not responsible for people falling in love.
Albert Einstein

A hundred hearts would be too few. To carry all my love for you.
Unknown

✳

Oh, if it be to choose and call thee mine, love, thou art every day my Valentine! Thomas Hood

✳

Anyone can catch your eye, but it takes someone special to catch your heart. Unknown

✳

The most important things are the hardest to say, because words diminish them. Stephen King

✳

*For 'twas not into my ear you whispered
But into my heart
'Twas not my lips you kissed
But my soul.* Judy Garland

✳

If I had a single flower for every time I think about you, I could walk forever in my garden. Attributed to Claudia Ghandi

✳

If I could reach up and hold a star for every time you've made me smile, the entire evening sky would be in the palm of my hand.
Unknown

✳

The most beautiful view is the one I share with you. Unknown

✳

When love is not madness, it is not love.
Pedro Calderon de la Barca

✳

Are we not like two volumes of one book?
Marceline Desbordes-Valmore

Engagement

How happy you both must be. Congratulations.

✳

The very warmest wishes. May both of you
enjoy this day of happy celebrations.

✳

We see the magic in both of you. Congratulations
and looking forward to your special day.

✳

Love always as you set out on life together.

✳

Congratulations on your engagement and all the best for your
wedding day and your future together.

✳

Congratulations on your engagement. May God's blessings
be upon you both as you prepare for your life together.

✳

Congratulations and good wishes for your future.
Support and love always.

✳

May you have the best of life together - true happiness is a
treasure more precious than diamonds.

✳

There are preparations to be made.
Enjoy the lead-up to your special day.

✳

A ring on her finger—vows to be made -
not much longer until your special day.

✳

We wish you all the happiness in the world together and
hope that all your dreams come true.

Wishing you both a lifetime of joy and happiness.

✱

We hope your lives together will be happy
and your plans to wed go smoothly.

✱

The adorable couple, [name] and [name]

✱

Praying God's very best for you both.

✱

Wishing you a bright future filled with happiness.

✱

Congratulations on the exciting news.

✱

Hoping your future holds lots of wonderful surprises and experiences.

✱

Our wish is that your future brings the very best of everything.

✱

Wishing you love and luck for the plans that lie ahead.
May your future together be bright.

✱

With fondest love and heartfelt congratulations to both of you.

✱

May your joy together be timeless.

✱

May your plans, dreams and preparations for a new life together
run smoothly. Have a wonderful engagement day.

✱

May your love, friendship and respect for each other
continue to grow as your big day approaches.

Wishing you love and romance.

＊

May the months and years ahead be filled with much joy,
happiness and excitement.

＊

Congratulations, our highest hopes for this exciting and joy-filled year.

＊

We love you and would be so happy if we could help you in any way.

＊

May your engagement be the beginning of a fairytale that
ends with 'Happily Ever After'.

＊

You're a match made in heaven. Congratulations.

＊

When things start to get crazy as you prepare for your wedding day,
look back and remember the love you shared on this engagement day.

＊

To a very special couple ... you make a perfect pair.

＊

It's no surprise ... you were made for each other. Congratulations.

＊

We hope that all your dreams come true and wish for your future
happiness and days filled with joy.

[We/I] had no doubt that yours was a love of a lifetime...
congratulations

＊

Yours is a bond that will last forever.

No doubt you are a perfect match.
We're only surprised it took so long. You belong together... congrats.

It couldn't have happened to a more perfect couple...congratulations.

Forever savour the joy of togetherness.

Glad to see you are finally taking the plunge. Couldn't be happier for you both.

Fantastic news. We knew the two of you would be inseparable. Congratulations on your engagement.

Wishing you love, luck and laughter in your future together.

May God bless you both as you embark on a journey of a lifetime. I'm sure the ride will be sweet.

May your love and friendship link you together eternally.

So thrilled to hear of your commitment. Looking forward to the day you say 'I do'.

*

May your special day sparkle with love and laughter. Wishing you years of contentment and joy.

Quotes

Love one another and you will be happy.
It's as simple and as difficult as that.
Michael Leunig

✳

Love is the expansion of two natures in such fashion that each include the other, each is enriched by the other. Felix Adler

✳

An engaged woman is always more agreeable than a disengaged. She is satisfied with herself. Her cares are over, and she feels that she may exert all her powers of pleasing without suspicion. All is safe with a lady engaged; no harm can be done. Jane Austen

✳

The person who tries to live alone will not succeed as a human being. His heart withers if it does not answer another heart. His mind shrinks away if he hears only the echoes of his own thoughts and finds no other inspiration. Pearl S Buck

✳

My mother says I didn't open my eyes for eight days after I was born, but when I did, the first thing I saw was an engagement ring. I was hooked. Elizabeth Taylor

✳

When you realise you want to spend the rest of your life with somebody, you want the rest of your life to start as soon as possible. Harry in the film *When Harry Met Sally*

✳

Long engagements give people the opportunity of finding out each other's character before marriage, which is never advisable.
Oscar Wilde

✳

Love is friendship set on fire. Jeremy Taylor

As you start out together
Along life's busy road
Remember, bring your dreams with you,
They lighten every load.
And then you will discover
As your journey starts today
That happiness walks with you
Hand-in-hand along the way.
Unknown

Love is a miracle, sweet as can be,
That will always remain a complete mystery.
For though it is something that's centuries old,
It cannot be purchased for silver or gold.
But instead must be given of one's own free will,
And received with no promises it must fulfil.
And once it's exchanged in this time-honoured way,
There's nothing that love cannot manage to say.
No problem's too great and no problem's too small,
For love, like a miracle, conquers them all.
And leaves in their place such a feeling of peace,
That joy, just like love, cannot help but increase!
Unknown

Whatever souls are made of, his and
mine are the same. Emily Brontë

In the arithmetic of love, one plus one equals everything, and two
minus one equals nothing. Mignon McLaughlin

True love stories never have endings. Richard Bach

My heart to you is given:
Oh, do give yours to me;
We'll lock them up together,
And throw away the key. Frederick Saunders

✳

Gravitation is not responsible for people falling
in love. Albert Einstein

✳

The loving are the daring. Bayard Taylor

✳

He felt now that he was not simply close to her, but that he did
not know where he ended and she began. Leo Tolstoy

✳

A girl loves a boy's voice when it has a ring in it. Unknown

Kitchen Tea

I hope you will find a use for this gift in your new kitchen.
May you spend many happy hours there.

✻

All the best for success in the kitchen.

✻

I am sure this will come in handy. Have a lovely kitchen tea.

✻

I hope you have many happy days in your kitchen with friends and family.

✻

May your kitchen be a haven of love and comfort
for you and your new family.

✻

The kitchen is the heart of the home. May it be so in yours.

✻

May the many hours you spend in your kitchen be filled
with love, laughter and eating.

✻

Wishing you both many happy memories of cooking triumphs and disasters as you spend time together in the heart of the home.

✻

Praying that the times you share in the kitchen are an
adventure and not a chore.

✻

Season your kitchen with love.

✻

Hoping you discover more about each other as you spend time
together in the kitchen, cooking, eating and cleaning up.

✻

Enjoy your time in the kitchen together. Remember to love
and cook with wild abandon.

Kitchens are a place for families to come together.

✳

May the main ingredient in your kitchen be love.

✳

A kitchen tea is a special time; spending time with those you love and learning kitchen wisdom from those who have gone before you. Enjoy your day.

✳

May your kitchen be a place of warmth where your family will come together and bond over meals made with love.

✳

Ensure your kitchen is not just for cooking and eating, but also for sharing and laughing.

Quotes

'Warm kitchen, warm friends.'
—Czech saying

✳

'When the stomach is full, the heart is glad.'
—Dutch proverb

✳

The kitchen: where food, fun, love and laughter and wild plans come together. Unknown

✳

One of the delights of life is eating with friends, second to that is talking about eating. And, for an unsurpassed double whammy, there is talking about eating while you are eating with friends.
Laurie Colwin in her book *Home Cooking*

✳

We may live without friends; we may live without books, but civilised men cannot live without cooks. Edward G Bulweri Lytton

There is no spectacle on earth more appealing than that of a beautiful woman in the act of cooking dinner for someone she loves. Thomas Wolfe

✻

In the childhood memories of every good cook, there's a large kitchen, a warm stove, a simmering pot and a Mum.
Barbara Costikyan

✻

There is one thing more exasperating than a spouse who can cook and won't, and that's a spouse who can't cook and will. Unknown

✻

Kitchen Rules: There's no such things as girl's work or boy's work— there's just work and it has to get done. Unknown

✻

Cooking is like love. It should be entered into with abandon or not at all. Harriet Van Horne

✻

A messy kitchen is a happy kitchen and this kitchen is delirious.
Unknown

✻

If God had intended us to follow recipes, He wouldn't have given us grandmothers. Linda Henley

✻

Worries go down better with soup. Jewish Proverb

✻

A good cook is like a sorceress who dispenses happiness.
Elsa Schiaparelli

✻

What is patriotism but the love of the food one ate as a child?
Lin Yutang

Crumbs of happiness... make a loaf of contentment. Unknown

✳

One of the very nicest things about life is the way we must regularly stop whatever it is we are doing and devote our attention to eating.
Luciano Pavarotti and William Wright, Pavarotti, My Own Story

✳

Approach love and cooking with reckless abandon. Unknown

✳

Kiss the cook and then take her out to dinner. Unknown

✳

When baking, follow directions. When cooking, go by your own taste. Laiko Bahrs

✳

An empty belly is the best cook. Estonian Proverb

✳

Bless the cook who serves love and laughter. Unknown

✳

A stack of dirty dishes is not a sign of a neglected house. It's a sign that the people who live here like to eat. Unknown

Marriage

*'God, the best maker of all marriages,
Combine your hearts into one.'*
—William Shakespeare (1564—1616),
Henry V

Congratulations. Best wishes for a lifetime of
love, happiness and special memories.

✳

The very warmest wishes and sincere congratulations.
May both of you enjoy your day of happy celebrations.

✳

Congratulations. Even though I'm on the other side
of the world, news still travels quickly.

✳

Congratulations on your marriage. We wish you much
happiness and that all your dreams come true.

✳

Congratulations on your marriage and we know God will
bless you through your many happy years together.

✳

Congratulations. It's wonderful to see you getting married as
you are perfectly suited—have a fantastic life together.

✳

Trust each other and you will be loyal; treat each other greatly
and you will each show yourselves great.

✳

It was once said that life can only be understood backwards, but it must be
lived forwards. May you go forward in leaps and bounds in your life
together.

✳

May your life together be a time in which you prosper,
your friends are true and happiness is assured.

✳

May your love for each other and the dreams that you
share be a huge part of your lives.

May your happiness and love for each other grow deeper
each day and make your lives together wonderful.

✳

May you share true contentment as husband and wife
each day of your life.

✳

May you always be lovers, but most of all friends.
Congratulations on your happy day.
May the joy of your love grow deeper with each anniversary.

✳

Our very best wishes for your wedding day
—long may the magic continue.

✳

May the Lord bless you richly in your new life together.
Look to him in every situation.

✳

Praying God's very best for you both.

✳

God bless you both richly on this special day.

✳

Love always, as you set out on a life together.

✳

This card comes with wishes for a happy day
and a happy life together.

✳

Wishing you both a lifetime of joy and happiness.

✳

May your life together be filled with happiness.

✳

Wishing you all the joy and happiness that marriage brings.

The adorable couple—enjoy the wonderful commitment you have made.

✳

We wish you all the happiness that life can bring your way.

✳

May your lives together hold everything you're dreaming of.

✳

You don't marry someone you can live with. You marry someone you can't live without. Congratulations.

✳

Congratulations. We know this is the beginning of a wonderful success story.

✳

Don't forget your individuality as you unite together as one, those qualities that make each of you special and are why you fell in love.

✳

Love each other, talk to each other but most of all forgive each other; then the journey will be sweet.

✳

We couldn't have asked for a better way to spend our day—being witness to the beginning of a great love story. Congratulations.

✳

We are so glad we are able to share this special day with you. You are the perfect couple and we know this is just the beginning of a beautiful journey as you travel life's road together.

✳

We know the build-up to the ceremony can be exhausting, so here's hoping you survived ... have a wonderful day and a fantastic honeymoon. Enjoy each other.

Wishing you all that love and life together has to offer ... as the years
progress, may your love and the joys you experience deepen.

✳

We are so happy to celebrate your transition from best friends to soul
mates ... Wishing you a beautiful future full of love,
laughter and prosperity.

✳

May this day bring to you all your dreams and all the gifts
on your bridal registry!

✳

As you embark on this new journey together, may your path be filled
with new beginnings leading to a fulfilling future.

✳

A match made in heaven ... We know your dreams
will all come true ... Congratulations.
May your marriage be a lifetime of joie de vivre.

✳

May this treasured day turn into a golden memory.
Wishing you lots of love, joy and happiness.

✳

Yay! We are so happy for you both. May God bless you as you make a
commitment to each other, to love one another.

✳

A loving marriage has a bond of immeasurable strength.
Wishing you a long and wonderful future together.

✳

Congratulations on a perfect match. May the freshness of your love
never grow old.

✳

May your lives together be rich with an abundance
of joy and love.

May the love that brought you together continue to grow so that you might be happier than you could have ever imagined.

✳

The guiding hand of God has brought you together that you may spend your lives together being fruitful and loved.

✳

May you continue to fall in love over and over again as you make special memories throughout your marriage.

✳

So today you're 'gettin' hitched!' We wish you all the best for your future together.

✳

Marriage is a beautiful occasion to celebrate the love and commitment you have to each other. Thank you for including us on your special day.

✳

May your happiness and love for each other grow with each day of your marriage. And may the sweetness of romance fill your hearts with joy.

✳

Always treat each other with compassion and tenderness, and nothing that the world sends your way will ever rock the foundation of your marriage.

✳

Laugh together often, and enjoy the times you share with just the two of you cocooned away from the world.

✳

May the love that led you to this special day continue to guide you through your future together.

✳

May the beautiful magic of this day bring you a long and joyous marriage.

Be happy, be loving, be kind
Be true and you will be forever.

*

Marriage is a promise of a lifetime together.
We look forward to hearing all about it in fifty years.

*

May the joy of your special day continue to radiate in your lives long
after the day is done.

*

May your wedding day fill your lives with joy, your home with laughter
and your marriage with love.

*

This day is the beginning of a wonderful journey that only brings you
closer together.

*

So glad we could share this special occasion with you.
May your love for one another grow deeper and deeper with every
passing year.

*

We know this wedding day is just the beginning to a
happy ever after.

Marriage Quotes

....

*'Marriage is an authentic weaving together of families, of two
souls with their individual fates and destinies, of time and
eternity—everyday life married to the timeless mysteries of the
soul.'*
Thomas Moore (1478—1535), English statesman and author

*

'In all of the wedding cake, hope is the sweetest of plums.'
Douglas Jerrold (1803—57), English dramatist and writer

'Ever wonder why God gives us two? A right hand to show the left what to do. One ear to listen and one to hear the problems of others, their laughter and fears. One eye to watch and one to behold the beautiful treasures that life has to hold. One foot to travel and one to stand tall. Two feet to land on if we should fall. One man to stand by a woman's side; one woman to cherish being his bride. The love between partners comes shining through, and that is the reason God has made two. May God bless you on your wedding day.'
Unknown

✳

'Marriage is love personified.'
Phoenix Flame, unknown

✳

'Marriage is the perfection of what love aimed at, ignorant of what it sought.'
Ralph Waldo Emerson (1803–82), US essayist and poet

✳

'Marriage—a book of which the first chapter is written in poetry and the remaining chapters written in prose.'
Beverly Nichols (1898–1983), British author

✳

'One should believe in marriage as in the immortality of the soul.'
Honoré de Balzac (1799–1850), French novelist

✳

'When you make a sacrifice in marriage, you're sacrificing not to each other but to unity in a relationship.'
Joseph Campbell (1904–87), US writer

✳

'Marriage is not a simple love affair, it's an ordeal, and the ordeal is the sacrifice of ego to a relationship in which two have become one.'
Joseph Campbell (1904–87), US writer

'True it is that marriages be done in heaven and performed on Earth.'
William Painter (c. 1540–94), British author

✳

'Marriage is our last, best chance to grow up.'
Joseph Barth, US clergyman

✳

'Married couples who love each other tell each other a thousand things without talking.'
Chinese proverb

✳

'There is no more lovely, friendly and charming relationship, communion or company than a good marriage.'
Martin Luther (1483–1586), German Protestant theologian

✳

'A good marriage is that in which each appoints the other guardian of his solitude.'
Rainer Maria Rilke (1875–1926), German poet and author

✳

'What God hath joined together, let man not put asunder.'
Matthew 19:6

✳

The goal of marriage is not to think alike, but to think together. Unknown

✳

A successful marriage requires falling in love many times, always with the same person. Mignon McLaughlin

✳

The best is yet to be. Robert Browning

✳

You don't marry someone you can live with—you marry the person you cannot live without. Unknown

The success of marriage comes not in finding the 'right' person, but in the ability of both partners to adjust to the real person they inevitably realise they married. John Fischer

✳

It is sometimes essential for a husband and wife to quarrel—they get to know each other better. Goethe

✳

Ultimately the bond of all companionship, whether in marriage or in friendship, is conversation. Oscar Wilde

✳

The first duty of love is to listen. Paul Tillich

✳

As for the secret to staying married: My wife tells me that if I ever decide to leave, she is coming with me. Jon Bon Jovi

✳

There is nothing more admirable than two people who see eye-to-eye keeping house as man and wife, confounding their enemies, and delighting their friends. Homer, 9th century BC

✳

A married man should forget his mistakes; no use two people remembering the same thing. Duane Dewel

✳

Marriage is a partnership in which each inspire the other, and brings fruition to both of you.
Millicent Carey McIntosh

✳

A happy marriage is a long conversation which always seems too short. Andre Maurois

✳

The perfect wife is one who doesn't expect a perfect husband.
Unknown

My greatest wish for the two of you is that through the years your love for each other will so deepen and grow, that years from now you will look back on this day, your wedding day, as the day you loved each other the least. Wedding toast, to the Bride and Groom

✳

Some people like to spend, others like to save, unfortunately they tend to marry each other! Unknown

✳

Before marriage, a man will lie awake thinking about something you said; after marriage, he'll fall asleep before you finish saying it. Helen Rowland

✳

Courtship is like looking at the beautiful photos in a seed catalogue. Marriage is what actually comes up in your garden. Unknown

✳

In marriage, every day you love, and every day you forgive. It is an ongoing sacrament, love and forgiveness. Bill Moyers

✳

There is no more lovely, friendly and charming relationship, communion or company than a good marriage. Martin Luther

✳

If you are losing an argument with your spouse, try a kiss. Unknown

✳

Give your husband an inch and he'll think he's a ruler. Unknown

✳

Just think: if it weren't for marriage, men would go through life thinking they had no faults at all. Unknown

Compromise in marriage is an amiable arrangement between husband and wife whereby they agree to let her have her own way. Unknown

✳

Love is blind... but marriage opens your eyes. Unknown

✳

Getting a husband is like buying an old house. You don't see it the way it is but the way it's going to be when you get it remodelled.
Barbara Johnson

✳

The secret to having a good marriage is to understand that marriage must be total, it must be permanent and it must be equal. Frank Pittman

✳

I have learned that only two things are necessary to keep one's wife happy. First, let her think she's having her own way. And second, let her have it. Lyndon B. Johnson

✳

The sum which two married people owe to one another defies calculation. It is an infinite debt, which can only be discharged through all eternity.
Johann Wolfgang von Goethe

✳

Don't go to bed angry. Stay up and fight! Unknown

Anniversary

One rose for one lover; one friend, one inspiration,
producing many special moments.

✳

As the years have passed, our love has not diminished—
may our togetherness never fade with age.

✳

The day we met I knew our love was meant to be.
The day we married I knew it was for eternity.

✳

Thank you for the years we have spent together.
I feel so wrapped in your love.

✳

May the years we have left be blessed.

✳

If we could go back in time, not a thing would
I change—fate brought us together.

✳

You are the light of my days. I belong in your arms,
surrounded with love.

✳

Sitting here thinking of you, remembering all the time, love and
happiness we have shared. Thank you for all you have given me.
I love you more every day.

✳

Being without you is like a day without chocolate.
Happy anniversary!

✳

Happy anniversary, darling! I'm the luckiest man in the world!

Forever and always—that's how long I'll love you. Happy anniversary.

✳

You showed me love,
You made me feel whole,
You gave me happiness,
You make me complete.

✳

Happy anniversary, sweetheart! I'm the luckiest woman in the world!

✳

Anniversaries come and go, but our love continues forever.

✳

To my husband/wife—you are my sweetheart, my confidant
and adviser, my comforter and friend. You are my happy place
away from the rest of the world. Happy anniversary!

✳

To the one I love on our anniversary … words will never be
able to express all I hold within my heart. You've made every
moment a happy memory. Happy anniversary!

I was lucky to find my true love and best friend when I met you.
Thank you for every year we have been together. Each year I fall
more in love with you … Happy Anniversary.

✳

How did I get so lucky? It must have been fate, to win the
heart of my soul mate.

✳

To my love bird … what a pair we make.

✳

Still in love after all this time … who would have thought?
I didn't think, I knew, because I've always loved you.

May our special journey together never end ...
from here to eternity, all my love.

✳

As the years go by the sweet memories accumulate. Not one will
ever be forgotten. Happy Anniversary my love.

✳

As we have shared and given over the years, my love has grown
deeper.

✳

The foundation of our love is so stable ... we were built to last.

✳

May the happiness we share today be ours tomorrow and forever.

✳

Ours is a match made in heaven ... Happy Anniversary.

✳

To my love everlasting. Happy Anniversary.

✳

The honeymoon continues.

✳

A day to look back on all we have shared and to look forward with
anticipation to our future together.

✳

Step by step—together—year by year.

✳

Every year I can look back and say it was better for having
you in it. Happy Anniversary.

✳

Our love started so quickly and has grown ever stronger over our time
together. It will last for eternity.

Wonderful years and memories to reminisce over, and the beginning of another year to come. Congratulations on a wonderful and lasting love.

✳

I know tomorrow will be wonderful simply because you are in it. Happy Anniversary.

✳

Everyday I fall in love... with you.

✳

Time flies when you're having fun!

✳

Somehow we pull it off... every year just gets better and better and I find myself more in love with you.

✳

Today we celebrate another year together standing firm on a foundation of trust, respect and love.

✳

It does not matter what I do each day or what challenges I face, all that matters is that you are right beside me.

✳

Our wedding was (number) years ago and I have not stopped celebrating.

✳

Wake me up, I must be dreaming. A love like ours is too good to be true.

✳

The best thing that has ever happened to me was when you married me. Thank you for all the years we have shared.

✳

I know they say marriage is hard work but I disagree. We love one another and that is all I need to be happy.

We have had our ups and downs, good times and bad. But through it all I have never doubted that we were meant to be together. I will love you forever.

✳

No one understands me like you do. Thank you for loving and accepting me unconditionally for all these years.

To another couple on their anniversary

Love brought you together as husband and wife ... and gave each of you a best friend for life. Happy anniversary.

✳

May your heart be filled with love and your life with happiness. Happy anniversary.

✳

May you always be warmed by each other's smile,
Always take time to walk and talk a while,
Always know deep down you're each other's best friend,
And enjoy the kind of love that grows and knows no end.
Happy anniversary.

✳

May the warmth and love you bring to others surround you both on your special day.

✳

'Music is love in search of a word.' You make such beautiful music together. Happy anniversary!

✳

You have proved that love conquers everything.

✳

[Number] years and still going strong. Have a fabulous day.

May today be filled with happy memories of the past and bright hopes for the future. Happy anniversary to a wonderful couple.

✱

God gave you both a special love to share ... because he knew how much you would cherish it. Happy anniversary.

✱

To a couple who really takes romance to heart. Have a wonderful day.

✱

To a beautiful pair on the birthday of your love affair.
Happy anniversary.

✱

We have seen the happiness that fills the home you've made.
Happy Anniversary

Your difference is what makes your love unique.
Congratulations on your anniversary.

✱

Faithful friends and partners. You're an inspiration to us all.

✱

Another year of a beautiful marriage. We have learned so much from you as you have worked to make your love last.

✱

Your love has stood the test of time, no matter what has come your way. You are both such an inspiration. Happy anniversary.

✱

It's such a joy to know two people so in love!
Happy anniversary to the special couple.

✱

There's no need to think about a second honeymoon—when there's no evidence that you have even finished your first! Happy anniversary.

Scientists have discovered that the longer people stay married, the more they begin to look alike. You'd better start wearing name tags. Happy anniversary.

*

When I look at you together, I think if only everyone could be so lucky. Happy Anniversary.

*

To a very special couple ... May this year be the happiest yet ... Warm wishes.

*

No-one is that good at acting—it must be the real thing. Your love for each other grows and it shows. Happy Anniversary.

*

Today we celebrate the love that was destined to be: the love of (name) and (name). Best wishes for your eternal future together.

*

May your love continue to flourish as you grow together. You are both so special to us. Happy Anniversary.

*

When a marriage radiates love like yours, you know you are truly blessed.

*

They say that after years together couples start to look alike ... so true. To a handsome couple ... Happy Anniversary.

*

Still in love after all this time. Congratulations on your everlasting love.

*

To Mum and Dad. You have taught [us/me] so much about relationships through your daily displays of patience, understanding, communication and sacrifice. Happy Anniversary.

I know that the love you share is growing each year. Congratulations on such a wonderful and rare marriage.

✻

To the most beautiful couple in all the land:
Congratulations on another wonderful year together.

✻

Happy Anniversary. May your marriage continue to be blessed with abundant love, joy and companionship.

✻

The seasons change and every day brings something new, but it is reassuring to know that a relationship like yours will last a lifetime.

✻

No one is perfect but you two are a perfect match.
Happy Anniversary.

✻

Thank you for being such great role models of how a marriage should be. Happy Anniversary.

✻

Each year together is unique with new adventures and experiences. Wishing you many more wonderful years together.

✻

Some things are always changing ... fashion, morals, the price of gas. But you two always stay the same. Please never change.

Anniversary Quotes

'Love seems the swiftest, but it is the slowest of all growths.
No man or woman really knows what perfect love is until
they have been married a quarter of a century.'
Mark Twain (1835–1910), US author and humorist

'With 50 years between you and your well-kept wedding vow,
the Golden Age, old friends of mine, is not a fable now.'
John Greenleaf Whittier (1807–92), US poet

✳

Coming together is the beginning. Keeping together is progress.
Working together is success. Henry Ford

✳

The development of a really good marriage is not a natural
process. It is an achievement. David and Vera Mace

✳

A wedding anniversary is the celebration of love, trust,
partnership, tolerance and tenacity. The order varies for any given
year. Paul Sweeney

✳

To keep your marriage brimming,
With love in the loving cup,
Whenever you're wrong, admit it;
Whenever you're right, shut up. Ogden Nash

✳

Our anniversary is a time to look back at the good times and a
time to look ahead to live our dreams together.
Catherine Pulsifer

✳

Our wedding was many years ago.
The celebration continues to this day. Gene Perret

✳

The most wonderful of all things in life, I believe, is the discovery
of another human being with whom one's relationship has a
growing depth, beauty and joy as the years increase. This inner
progressiveness of love between two human beings is a most
marvellous thing; it cannot be found by looking for it or by
passionately wishing for it. It is a sort of divine accident, and the
most wonderful of all things in life. Hugh Walpole, Sr.

Love is just a word until someone comes along and gives it meaning. Chuck Palahniuk

✻

If I know what love is, it is because of you. Herman Hesse

✻

The bonds of matrimony are like any other bonds—they mature slowly. Peter De Vries

✻

My most brilliant achievement was my ability to be able to persuade my wife to marry me. Winston Churchill

✻

*I wouldn't change a thing
as happiness you bring.
You are my soul mate.
A marriage made by fate.* Catherine Pulsifer

✻

Chains do not hold a marriage together. It is threads, hundreds of tiny threads, which sew people together through the years. Simone Signoret

✻

The best love is the kind that awakens the soul and makes us reach for more; that plants a fire in our hearts and brings peace to our minds... That's what you've given me and that's what I hope to give to you forever. From the movie *The Notebook* (2004)

✻

Let the wife make the husband glad to come home, and let him make her sorry to see him leave. Martin Luther

New Baby

*'A baby was created
by the hand of God above,
To give the world the sweetest touch
of tenderness and love.'*

Unknown

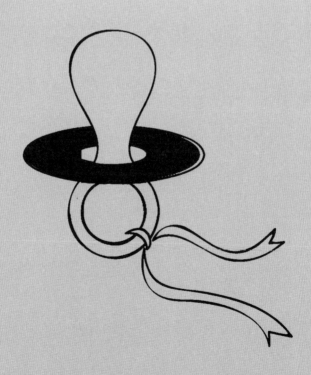

Our congratulations on the birth of your son/daughter.
We are very happy for you and wish you all the best.

✳

Congratulations on the arrival of your new daughter/son.
May God richly bless him/her always.

✳

Congratulations on your new arrival! Just remember—
babies are subject to change without notice!

✳

Welcome to the night shift! The hours are lousy, but
the benefits are great! Congratulations on your new baby.

✳

Congratulations on the arrival of [name].
We were so excited to hear your news.

✳

Congratulations on the birth of your new little baby.
Wishing you lots of fun times together as a family.

✳

Congratulations on your new baby. He/she has such beautiful
little fingers. You'll soon be wrapped around them.

✳

We were so pleased to hear everything went well
for you and your new little baby.

✳

Congratulations to you both and I hope
the little fella gives you years of joy.

✳

Congratulations on the first of many.

✳

Our love and thoughts are with you all on this wonderful event.

May God richly bless you as you begin parenthood together.
We know that every day ahead of you will be the happiest kind.

*

Congratulations on your 'Bundle of Joy'.

*

At last he/she has arrived. Congratulations to you both.

*

Glory be to God for the safe arrival of [name].
I am sure he/she will bring much joy to your hearts.

*

You know what they say about babies—it's just one
damp thing after another! Congratulations.

*

Dear Mummy and Daddy. Thank you for my baby sister/brother.
Love [name].

*

This gift was purchased with much excitement on the birth of your
baby son/daughter [name]. With much love and congratulations.

*

Your new baby is so blessed to have such fabulous
parents with so many wonderful qualities.

*

The birth of your new son/daughter deserves the greatest celebration—
the very best wishes for your future together.

*

Congratulations. May [name] bring you both all
the happiness in the world.
Dear [name]. Welcome. It's good to see you at last.

*

Congratulations on the birth of [name]. May the Lord bless you with
peace, happiness, health and safety.

Congratulations on the birth of your little boy/girl. You must be very proud and overwhelmed. I wish you all a future full of love and happy memories.

✳

Congratulations on the birth of your beautiful son/daughter. I know he/she will bring you many cherished memories.

✳

A huge congratulations on your [weight] [name] . He/she is just adorable.

✳

We are very happy for you both. Congratulations to the proud parents and grandparents.

✳

Congratulations. Look after the baby and yourself too.

✳

Congratulations on your new bundle of love, small enough to hold in your arms, yet big enough to fill your whole life with joy.

✳

Congratulations. You guys did an excellent job. We look forward to spending time with your growing family in the years ahead.

✳

We pray all God's goodness for your little family. May he guide you as parents and keep you all safe and well. Thank goodness for disposables.

✳

Congratulations, you must be filled with joy. Our love to you both and your new little boy/girl.

✳

The wonder of a new baby is the greatest gift of all.

May your new son/daughter always be cradled in
love and blessed with every happiness.

✳

A big welcome to baby [name]. May each new
day bring new discoveries and surprises.

✳

Congratulations on your new baby, the first of many I'm sure. May this
child open a whole new world of love, laughter and sleepless nights.
May the Lord bless you greatly as a family and fill you both with
his strength, joy and wisdom for all the exciting times ahead.

✳

We were delighted to hear of your successful productions. Well done.

✳

Congratulations. May you share the fun and work together.

✳

Congratulations on the arrival of your beautiful bundle of joy [name].
With all our love and best wishes.

✳

Congratulations on the new arrival to [address].

✳

The months of anticipation are finally over and
the months of sleep deprivation ahead.

✳

Wishing you all the best things for the new
little boy/girl who's just joined your family.

✳

You have a son/daughter [name]. That's fantastic.
Congratulations to you and love to your little boy/girl.

✳

Congratulations on your little baby boy/girl [name].
Take care of him/her. It's a jungle out there.

[name] will fill your days with laughter and love and your home with joy. With love to the happy family.

✳

Congratulations. We know you will find real love and joy seeing your little son/daughter grow.

✳

I once heard the best way to give advice to your children is to find out what they want and then advise them to do it. Happy parenting.

It doesn't matter what they say: your life is about to change … for the better. Congratulations.

✳

Glad to hear there is a beautiful new face to light up the world.

✳

So happy to hear that [baby's name] arrived safe and sound. Congratulations.

✳

Dear [baby's name], you have the best parents in the world. I look forward to seeing you grow into the amazing person you are destined to be.

✳

The cutest fingers, the cutest toes, the sweetest lips and button nose.

✳

Just remember … the overwhelming tiredness fades when you hear those first coos, see that first smile and feel those tiny fingers wrapped around yours. Congratulations, it's all worth it.

✳

Congratulations on your new precious gift, a life to nurture.

✳

May the ensuing months be filled with sweet and uninterrupted dreams for the whole family.

How amazing is this new love you feel for this beautiful gift
from God ... Congratulations.

✳

As your heart fills with love, may your days fill with happiness.

✳

May you savour the miracle of this new life entrusted to you.
You will both be wonderful parents.

✳

A star is born that will light up your lives.

✳

Enjoy every minute they are awake, but when they go to sleep ...
YOU need to sleep.

✳

Soon you will see a smile that will forever melt your heart.

✳

Welcome, [baby's name], into the hearts of all your family
who will always love you.

✳

Hey baby, welcome to the world.

✳

Coochee coochee coo, ga ga, goo goo. Welcome to baby talk.
Congratulations.

Now you've gone and done it!.... Changed your life forever for the
better. Congratulations on the birth of [name].

✳

No matter what happens for the rest of your life, you will always
cherish this moment when you brought a new life into the world.

✳

How wonderful is the smell of a newborn... don't you wish you could
bottle it.

A new baby brings so much joy and captivates your heart in a way you could never imagine. Congratulations on your new addition.

*

A new baby brings such joy. May you hold onto this joy in your heart as you hold him/her in your arms.

*

A dream come true. Congratulations on the much anticipated arrival of little [name].

*

Sending you a bundle of love on the arrival of your new little bundle of joy.

*

Hello [name], I am so excited to welcome you into the world and to watch you grow into the wonderful person you are destined to be.

*

Ten little fingers, ten small toes and one tiny little button nose. Congratulations on the birth of [name].

*

I hear there is a new girl/boy in town. Congratulations on the arrival of [name].

*

A new baby equals a new challenge. Wishing you an abundance of patience and stamina... you're going to need it.

*

You have been entrusted with a most valuable treasure and I have no doubt you will be awesome parents.
Congratulations on the arrival of your little boy/girl.

*

With parents like you, [name]'s got nothing but a future of fabulous possibilities. Enjoy being parents for the first time and savour every minute. Congratulations

Sometimes the responsibility of bringing a little person into the world and helping them to find their way is a little daunting. But I have no doubt you will make wonderful parents to [name].

✳

Now you will know love in a way that neither of you will have ever known before. Blessings to you and your new little family.

✳

We can't wait to meet you baby [name]. I bet you are super cute just like your brothers/sisters.

✳

Wonderful news! All the best as you settle into your new life as a family of [number].

✳

[Name] is simply perfect!
Congratulations to your wonderful family.

✳

I have no doubt this baby is more wonderful than you could have ever imagined. And it won't be long until it's more trouble too!

✳

Another blessing from God and a sweet addition to your growing family. We look forward to meeting him/her very soon.

✳

Here is a phrase you are now going to have to commit to memory. It won't be long until you need it: 'Because I said so.'

✳

It's worth it ... every sleepless minute won't change the love you have for this new little person. Congratulations.

✳

For a short time you will forget how to sleep, talk and walk ... but it's all worth it. Congratulations.

Congratulations on becoming parents. May [name] be nothing but a
source of joy for you both.

✳

It has been said having a baby changes your life.
May all the changes be pleasant ones. Congrats.

✳

Congratulations. [I/We] look forward to getting to know
[name] as she/he grows day by day.

✳

If you didn't love your in-laws before you will now.
You will be begging them to come and visit just so you can have a
moment's sanity.

New Baby Quotes

'Another miracle in this world. Welcome.'
Unknown

✳

'Babies are such a nice way to start people.'
Unknown

✳

'Every child is born a genius.'
R. Buckminster Fuller (1895—1983), US inventor and author

✳

*'There are times when parenthood seems nothing
but feeding the mouth that bites you.'*
Peter De Vries (1910—93), US novelist

✳

'Blessed are the young for they shall inherit the national debt.'
Herbert Hoover (1874—1964), former US president

'Children are the only form of immortality that we can be sure of.'
Peter Ustinov (1921–2004), British actor

✳

'Parents are the bones upon which children sharpen their teeth.'
Peter Ustinov (1921–2004), British actor

✳

'A baby is God's opinion that the world should go on.'
Carl Sandburg (1878–1967), US writer

✳

A baby is born with a need to be loved—and never outgrows it.
Frank A Clark

✳

A baby is cuddles and tickles on toes,
The sweet scent of powder, a kiss on the nose! Unknown

✳

People who say they sleep like a baby usually don't have one.
Leo J Burke

✳

Making the decision to have a child is momentous. It is to decide
forever to have your heart go walking around outside your body.
Elizabeth Stone

✳

A new baby is like the beginning of all things—wonder, hope,
a dream of possibilities. Eda J Le Shan

✳

Life is filled with lots of things that make it all worthwhile,
but none is better than the love found in your baby's smile.
Unknown

✳

A baby will make love stronger, days shorter, nights longer,
bankroll smaller, home happier, clothes shabbier, the past
forgotten, and the future worth living for. Unknown

*If one feels the need of something grand, something infinite,
something that makes one feel aware of God, one need not go far
to find it. I think that I see something deeper, more infinite, more
eternal than the ocean in the expression of the eyes of a little
baby when it wakes in the morning and coos or laughs because it
sees the sun shining on its cradle.* Vincent Van Gogh

✻

A baby is an in-estimable blessing and a bother. Mark Twain

✻

*Having a baby changes the way you view your in-laws.
I love it when they come to visit.
They hold the baby and I go out.* Matthew Broderick

✻

*A baby changes your dinner party conversation from politics to
poops.* Maurice Johnston

✻

*A baby will make love stronger,
Days shorter, Nights longer,
Bankroll smaller, Clothes shabbier,
The past forgotten,
And the future worth living for.* Unknown

✻

*It was the tiniest thing I ever decided to
put my whole life into.* Terri Guillemets

✻

*When my kids become wild and unruly, I use a nice, safe playpen.
When they're finished, I climb out.* Erma Bombeck

✻

*Babies are always more trouble than you thought and more
wonderful.* Charles Osgood

✻

*Having a child is surely the most
beautifully irrational act that two people
in love can commit.* Bill Cosby

Christening

As you christen your beautiful baby, may God's blessings continue
to flow over you as you grow together as a family.

✶

It's (name's) Christening day. On this very special day, be filled with
pride as you look at your beautiful (daughter/son).

✶

Congratulations on this special day. Remember the words
of the Lord ... 'Behold, I am with you and will keep you
wherever you go ...' *The Bible*, Genesis 28:150

✶

On this day we send our best wishes and pray for a guardian angel to
watch over (name), to protect and guide (her/him) as they grow.

✶

Congratulations on this special day. We look forward to seeing you
grow into a beautiful person inside and out.

✶

We send best wishes on this day as (name) is baptised
before family and friends.

✶

Congratulations ... Wishing you beauty and happiness
for the rest of your life.

✶

On your Christening day, we thank God for the wonderful,
special miracle you are.

✶

We are so excited to be sharing this special day with you and look
forward to watching your little one fulfil (his/her) purpose.

✶

May (name) grow knowing they are loved by you and by God.

We celebrate with you today as this beautiful child is raised
in a family knowing God's love.

✳

We celebrate with you as you christen [name] into God's family.

✳

All creatures great and small, The Lord God loves them all.

✳

What a beautiful gift from God. God bless you both as you guide and
shape [name] with God's help.

✳

May [name]'s life be filled with blessing from heaven. We are
honoured to be invited to witness such a special occasion.

✳

May your christening day be filled with lots of love and happiness.
Blessings to you and your family.

✳

We wish your precious baby a blessed and charmed life.

✳

May God keep [name] forever in his care.

✳

Your beautiful baby shows the wonder of God and His creation.
Blessings to [name].

✳

May [name] be guided by God through the path He has for him/her
always.

✳

May you and little [name] experience the tenderness of God on this
special day.

✳

May [name] be kept safe in God's care throughout his/her life.

As you place your child into God's care forevermore, we look forward to watching [name] grow into the person they are destined to be.

✳

May God grant you an abundance of wisdom throughout your life. Much love on your Christening day.

✳

May God's abundant blessing light the path of baby [name] throughout his/her precious life.

✳

May this precious child from heaven above be welcomed into God's family with nothing but love.

✳

We celebrate with you today as you place your child in God's care forevermore.

✳

This child is a symbol of God's love. May He guide you both as you help him/her grow.

✳

Remember the words of the Lord Jesus Christ,
how he said, 'Let the children come to me,
do not hinder them; for to such belongs the kingdom of God.'
The Bible, Jude 1:17–19

✳

May the Lord give His angel charge over you, to guide you in all your ways. The Bible, Psalm 91:11

✳

If I had influence with the good fairy who is supposed to preside
over the christening of all children, I should ask that her gift to
each child in the world be a sense of wonder so indestructible that
it would last throughout life. Rachel Carson

Lord, bless this tiny infant,
Who is brought to you today,
And teach those precious little feet,
To follow in your way.
Lord, bless the baby's parents, too,
And with your loving care,
Grant them all the happiness,
A family can share.
Unknown

✳

A precious angel from heaven above will be welcomed
into God's family with love. Unknown

✳

I love these little people; and it is not a slight thing,
when they, who are so fresh from God, love us. Charles Dickens

✳

Now I lay me down to sleep,
I pray Thee, Lord, Thy child to keep:
Thy love guard me through the night
And wake me with the morning light. Prayer

✳

Every child born into the world is a new thought of God.
An ever fresh and radiant possibility. Kate Douglas Wiggins

✳

In praising or loving a child, we love and praise not that which is,
but that which we hope for. Goethe

✳

God grant your little one
all the blessing of His gentle love. Unknown

✳

From God's loving arms, to ours. Unknown

✳

Every child born into the world is a new thought of God, an ever
fresh and radiant possibility.
Kate Douglas Wiggins

Bar / Bat Mitzvah

We wish you eternal blessings as you continue to grow
and learn from the Torah

✳

The day is here. Mazal Tov.

✳

This holy celebration day will stay with you forever. Enjoy.

✳

You are now a young man/lady.
Cherish the memory of this holy celebration.

✳

May you be continually blessed with the wisdom
and love of the Torah

✳

Be proud of all you have achieved in the lead up to this day. Mazal Tov

✳

We are so proud of your commitment to your
faith and its traditions.

✳

As you wrap yourself in your talit, soak up fond
memories of your special day

✳

Whoever teaches his son teaches not only his son, but also his son's
son—and so on to the end of generations.
Talmud, Kiddushin 30a

✳

He who plants a tree plants a hope. Lucy Larcom

✳

*He shall be like a tree planted by waters sending forth its roots by
a stream.* Jeremiah 17: 8

I found a fruitful world, because my ancestors planted it for me.
Likewise I am planting for my children.
Talmud, Taanit 23a

✳

And the boy grew up and the Lord blessed him.
Judges 13: 24

✳

Train up a child in the way he should go and even when he is old
he will not depart from it. Proverbs 22: 6

✳

Sing and rejoice, daughter of Zion for, lo, I come, and will dwell in
your midst. Declares the Lord.
Zechariah 2: 14

✳

Incline thine ear, hear the words of the wise and apply thy heart
unto my knowledge. Proverbs 22: 17

Mother's Day

'When it comes to love, Mum's the word.'
—Unknown

Mum, you have been my inspiration. You have taught
me how to live and shown me how to love.

✻

All my good qualities I have learned from you.
Thank you for making me who I am.

✻

A mother's love is special. Thank you for always making me feel
special.

✻

Where you are will always be home. Our feet may leave it,
but never our hearts. Happy Mother's Day.

✻

You've always been there for me—
my mother, my mentor and my friend.

✻

Before becoming a mother, I had a hundred theories on how to bring
up
children. Now I have children and only one theory: love them,
especially when they least deserve to be loved. Thanks for all your love.
Happy Mother's Day.

✻

I love you, Mum—And this isn't the last time I'm going to tell you!
Happy Mother's Day.

✻

Mum, today's your day, so take it easy and relax.
You always seemed to know just what to do or what
to say to make my life so joyful and special.

✻

The precious moments you have given me
throughout my life will never be forgotten.

You gave me everything that has made me the person I am today.
Most of all, thank you for your unconditional love.

✻

Thank you for your loving kindness, your valuable wisdom
and your unconditional belief in me.

✻

In my heart, how could I ever forget my mother's love.
Your circle of love never ends.

✻

Thank you most of all for your love.

✻

There is no blessing quite so dear as a Mum like
you to love year after year! Happy Mother's Day.

✻

I just wanted to say how lucky I am to have a mother so beautiful
inside and out.

✻

Despite all of life's imperfections, you weave of it a world of joy and
wonder. With love on Mother's Day.

✻

To the best cookie-maker in the world.

✻

It's so hard for me to put together the words I want to say.
Just know that I love you this Mother's day.

✻

To my Mum, my friend, my confidant, happy Mother's Day.

✻

On Mother's Day, your children are supposed to cater to your every
whim—sort of goes against the natural order of things, doesn't it?
If only I could have experienced being a mother for a day when I was
a child I would have been a lot better behaved! Thanks for the
amazing patience you have always shown me.

Thank you for the influence you have been on my life. I don't know where or who I would be without you.

✳

I love that I can call you anytime, night or day, and you will know exactly what to say.

✳

I have learnt so much from your loving, compassionate and beautiful nature. You are my inspiration.

✳

Mum, you give me the courage and determination to go out into the world and face my fears and find success.

✳

Now that I have children of my own, I appreciate you a whole lot more. Sorry it took such a long time.

✳

Mum, thank you for guiding me each day with love and grace, building my strength and independence.

✳

I did not always agree with the things you said or did, but without your principles and love, I would not be the person I am today. Thank you.

✳

Because of you ... I can conquer the world.

✳

Thank you for standing by me and believing in me even when I was difficult. I could always count on your support to pull me through.

✳

To the most accomplished woman I know ... I am so proud to be your (daughter/son).

To the most important person in my life ...
I am proud to call you my Mum.

✳

The older I get the more I appreciate all that you are in my life.

✳

The dedication, understanding and patience you show me
will always be appreciated. Thanks for being there.

✳

Thank you for helping all my dreams come true.

✳

I could not have wished for a better mother. You are always there for
me with a hot cup of tea and never-ending words of wisdom.

✳

To the best mum ever. You are the best shopping companion I could
ever wish for. You cook the best food ever. Never short of good advice
and perhaps the most special person in my life.

✳

Though I may not always say it or act as though it true... you really
are the best mum ever!

✳

You mean the world to me. I don't know what I would do or where I
would be without you. Happy Mother's Day.

✳

Now that I have children of my own I realise what a terror I was.
Thankyou for your patience and loving me just as I am.

✳

Every day I appreciate you more and more. Your legacy will live forever
through generations to come.

✳

I know it cost you a lot to help me get to where I am today. Not just
money, but physical, mental and emotional expense as well.

Thankyou for all that you have invested in my life. I will always try to make you proud.

✳

Remember the first time I made you breakfast in bed? Well my cooking skills are yet to improve. I might be better at lunch or dinner in bed instead.

✳

Even when I was little you helped my dreams become reality. Thankyou for everything you have done.

✳

I was trying to think of one word to describe you and what you mean to me, but how could I pick just one?
You mean the world to me.

✳

When I was little I always wondered why there was not a children's day. Now I know that, thanks to you, every day was children's day. Which makes mother's day all the more special.

✳

To the most special and wonderful woman in my life.
Everyday I think of you with love and fondness.
To me everyday is mother's day.

✳

To my mum and role model. You taught me how to live and love. Thankyou for raising me, I hope I make you proud.

✳

I may be taller than you but you are still the bigger person. I will always have so much to learn from you. Thankyou for being my inspiration.

'All that I am or ever hope to be, I owe to my angel mother.'
Abraham Lincoln (1809–65), former US president

✳

'Of all the rights of women, the greatest is to be a mother.'
Lin Yutang (1895–1976), Chinese author

✳

'The most important thing a father can do for his children is to
love their mother.'
Unknown

✳

'A man loves his sweetheart the most, his wife the best,
but his mother the longest.'
Irish proverb

✳

'The heart of a mother is a deep abyss at the bottom of
which you will always find forgiveness.'
Honoré de Balzac (1799–1850), French novelist

✳

'By and large, mothers and housewives are the only workers who
do not have regular time off. They are the great vacationless class.'
Anne Morrow Lindbergh (1906–2001), US writer and aviator

✳

'The mother's heart is the child's schoolroom.'
Henry Ward Beecher (1813–87), US Congregational clergyman

✳

'Youth fades, love droops, the leaves of friendship fall;
a mother's secret hope outlives them all.'
Oliver Wendell Holmes (1809–94), US physician, poet and humorist

✳

'A mother understands what a child does not say.'
Jewish proverb

'Mother's love is peace. It need not be acquired,
it need not be deserved.'
Erich Fromm (1900–80), US psychoanalyst, born in Germany

*

'The hand that rocks the cradle is the hand that rules the world.'
William Ross Wallace (1819–81), US hymnwriter

'Her voice was ever soft, gentle and low, an excellent thing in a
woman.'
William Shakespeare (1564–1616), King Lear

*

'My mother was the most beautiful woman I ever saw.
All I am I owe to my mother. I attribute all my success in life
to the moral, intellectual and physical education I received from her.'
George Washington (1732–99), former US president

*

If at first you don't succeed, do it like your mother told you.
Unknown

*

My mother had a great deal of trouble with me, but I think she
enjoyed it. Mark Twain

*

Being a full-time mother is one of the highest salaried jobs in my
field, since the payment is pure love. Mildred B Vermont

*

She never quite leaves her children at home, even when she
doesn't take them along. Margaret Culkin Banning

*

The mother's heart is the child's schoolroom. Henry Ward Beecher

I love my mother as the trees love water and sunshine—she helps me grow, prosper, and reach great heights. Adabella Radici

*

A mother is a person who, seeing there are only four pieces of pie for five people, promptly announces she never did care for pie.
Tenneva Jordan

*

If evolution really works, how come mothers only have two hands?
Milton Berle

*

A suburban mother's role is to deliver children obstetrically once, and by car forever after. Peter De Vries

*

When you are a mother, you are never really alone in your thoughts. A mother always has to think twice, once for herself and once for her child.
Sophia Loren in her book *Women and Beauty*

*

Mother love is the fuel that enables a normal human being to do the impossible. Marion C Garretty, quoted in *A Little Spoonful of Chicken Soup for the Mother's Soul*

*

Now, as always, the most automated appliance in a household is the mother. Beverly Jones

*

The joys of motherhood are never fully experienced until the children are in bed. Unknown

*

*The sweetest sounds to mortals given
Are heard in Mother, Home, and Heaven.*
William Goldsmith Brown

My mom is a never-ending song in my heart of comfort, happiness and being. I may sometimes forget the words but I always remember the tune. Graycie Harmon

✳

All mothers are working mothers. Unknown

✳

I thought my mom's whole purpose was to be my mom. That's how she made me feel. Natasha Gregson Wagner

✳

There are two lasting bequests we can give our children. One is roots. The other is wings. Hodding Carter, Jr

✳

The heart of a mother is a deep abyss at the bottom of which you will always find forgiveness. Honore de Balzac

✳

Biology is the least of what makes someone a mother.
Oprah Winfrey

✳

We never know the love of the parent until we become parents ourselves. Henry Ward Beecher

✳

No matter how old a mother is, she watches her middle-aged children for signs of improvement.
Florida Scott-Maxwell

Father's Day

*'Blessed indeed is the man who hears
many gentle voices call him father!'*
—Lydia Maria Child (1802—80),
US abolitionist

You have made so many sacrifices for me. You are courageous, selfless and loving.

✳

The good qualities you have given me will always be in style.

✳

Thank you for your amazing love and strength,
which made our house a home.

✳

Your strength and courage was such an important part of my life during hard times.

✳

Thank you for forgiving me when I am wrong. Thank you for praising me when I am right. But, most of all, thank you for being there for me.

✳

Dad, you've always given me everything I wanted. Either that or you're very good at convincing me. Happy Father's Day.

✳

My Dad, my hero. Happy Father's Day.

✳

Happy Father's Day. I hope I've made you proud, Dad. And if not, hey, maybe you ought to lower your expectations.

✳

Hope, love and peace to you this Father's Day.

✳

Happy Father's Day. You've always issued the law in our house, Dad, and Mum carries it out. I guess that makes you an authority figurehead.

✳

Thank you for everything you have taught me.

✳

Not a day goes by that I don't feel loved by you.

✳

Dear Dad, you always know what is on my mind. You're patient
and helpful. Your love plays such a huge part in my life.

✳

Thank you for your love and support as I set out
to achieve my goals and dreams.

✳

You've always been a cut above the rest. Happy Father's Day.

✳

Each year that passes, I am more grateful that you are my Dad.

✳

You are the greatest man on Earth to me.
Thank you for keeping me grounded.

✳

Thank you for sharing all of life's lessons with me and teaching me
that hard work really does pay off. Happy Father's Day.

✳

Dad, as a tribute to you and your principles, I've always tried
to live my life by your time-honoured philosophy—
nothing's too good for my baby! Happy Father's Day.

✳

When I was little, Dad, I depended on you for my very existence. And
then I figured out how to turn the TV on myself. Happy Father's Day.

✳

Thank you for being my father. You have loved, protected
and guided me and I only hope I can be the father to my kids
that you have been to me.

✳

When I fell down, you picked me up ... When I was sad you made
me laugh ...When I was scared you comforted me ...
You're everything a Dad should be.

*

Thinking of you on this special day and the difference
your presence has made in my life.

*

Thanks for such a great start to life.

*

You showed me how to live honestly, lovingly and courageously.

*

Dad, you are always someone I will look up to no matter
how tall I grow.

*

Thank you for being the best example of 'how to live life'
a child could ask for.

*

Thanks for all the good times, Dad. I'm looking forward to many more.

*

Thank you for being the one I could always count on.

*

Your integrity sets you above the rest. I'm lucky to have such
a great role model.

*

Will I ever be able to fill your shoes? You are such an inspiration.

*

One word to describe my Dad ... ingenious.

*

To my father and friend, thankyou for your guidance and
encouragement.

On this day I just want to remind you of how much I respect you. You have taught me leadership while you showed me how much you care. I appreciate all you have taught me.

✷

Thank you for being a source of strength, for your understanding heart and for your readiness to help.

✷

I have so many wonderful memories from my childhood and I am dreaming of the wonderful moments yet to be had. Happy Father's Day.

✷

A day to celebrate all the happy memories we have created and shared over the years. Happy Father's Day.

✷

To the head honcho; man about the house; the one who wears the pants; the boss... Happy Father's Day.

✷

Even if I spent the rest of my life searching, I would never find a father as wonderful as you.

✷

You are Batman. You are Spiderman. You are Superman.
You are my hero.

✷

Thank you for making me laugh even when I was sad!
Thank you for being a shining light in my darkest night.
Thank you for being my Dad.

✷

I know I don't say it much, but how could we let this day go by without saying how much you mean to me. I love you Dad.

✷

Even in the midst of my successes, my failures and my shortcomings, you have always accepted me, just as I am.

I hope that someday I can come close to having your strength, your faith, your boldness and your wisdom. Just to be like you.

*

I am totally blessed to have the presence of a beautiful, wonderful, loving father. Thank you for bringing me into the world and being my Dad.

*

As I see my children growing I often look back to the things you taught me when I was a child. Even now I recognise that I am still, and will always be, your child.

*

Your principles and the way you conduct yourself have been the guiding force in my life. Thank you for being my guiding light.

'It is a wise father who knows his own child.'
William Shakespeare (1564–1616), *The Merchant of Venice*

✱

'It doesn't matter who my father was;
it matters who I remembered he was.'
Anne Sexton (1928–1974), US poet

✱

'One of the oldest human needs is having someone to wonder
where you are when you don't come home at night.'
Margaret Mead (1901–78), US anthropologist

✱

'A man should have a child, plant a tree and write a book.'
Chinese proverb

✱

He didn't tell me how to live; he lived,
and let me watch him do it. Clarence Budington Kelland

✱

I never had a chance to choose the man to be my Dad,
But I thank my lucky stars for the taste my mother had. Unknown
By the time a man realises that maybe his father was right, he
usually has a son who thinks he's wrong. Charles Wadworth

✱

Sometimes the poorest man leaves his children
the richest inheritance. Ruth E Renkel

✱

I love my father as the stars—he's a bright shining example
and a happy twinkling in my heart. Adabella Radici

✱

*A truly rich man is one whose children run into his arms
when his hands are empty.* Unknown

∗

*When I was a boy of 14, my father was so ignorant I could hardly
stand to have the old man around. But when I got to be 21, I was
astonished at how much he had learned in 7 years.*
Mark Twain in his memoir, Old Times on the Mississippi

∗

*I talk and talk and talk, and I haven't taught people in 50 years
what my father taught by example in one week.* Mario Cuomo

∗

*My father used to play with my brother and me in the yard.
Mother would come out and say, 'You're tearing up the grass.'
'We're not raising grass,' Dad would reply. 'We're raising boys.'*
Harmon Killebrew

∗

*Fatherhood is pretending the present you love most
is soap-on-a-rope.* Bill Cosby

∗

Father! To God himself we cannot give a holier name.
William Wordsworth

∗

A father carries pictures where his money used to be. Unknown
*Small boys become big men through the influence of big men
who care about small boys.* Unknown

∗

*The greatest gift I ever had
Came from God; I call him Dad!* Unknown

∗

I cannot think of any need in childhood as strong as the need for a father's protection. Sigmund Freud

✳

There's something like a line of gold thread running through a man's words when he talks to his daughter, and gradually over the years it gets to be long enough for you to pick up in your hands and weave into a cloth that feels like love itself.
John Gregory Brown in his book *Decorations in a Ruined Cemetery*

✳

A father is a banker provided by nature. French Proverb

✳

Any man can be a father but it takes someone special to be a dad.
Anne Geddes

✳

Some day I will find my prince but my Daddy will always be my King. Unknown

✳

A man's children and his garden both reflect the amount of weeding done during the growing season. Unknown

✳

'Fathers, like mothers, are not born. Men grow into fathers—and fathering is a very important stage in their development.
David M. Gottesman

✳

A father doesn't tell you that he loves you.
He shows you. Dimitri The Stoneheart

✳

My father gave me the greatest gift anyone could give another person, he believed in me. Jim Valvano

✳

Small boy's definition of Father's Day: It's just like Mother's Day only you don't spend so much. Unknown

The guys who fear becoming fathers don't understand that fathering is not something perfect men do, but something that perfects the man. Frank Pittman, *Man Enough*

Friendship

'I went outside to find a friend,
But could not find one there.
I went outside to be a friend,
And friends were everywhere.'
—Unknown

Many people come in and out of my life, but only true friends leave footprints in my heart! Thank you for being a great friend.

✻

Thank you for being a genuine friend ... one who is not afraid to say things, out of love, that are hard to say and hard to hear but cares enough to speak up.

✻

You are a true friend.
We cry through the bad times,
we laugh through the good ...
with happiness and smiles,
with pain and tears,
I know you will be with me
throughout the years.

✻

Thank you for being a true friend. You have overlooked my weaknesses and encouraged me in my strengths. Thank you for accepting me just as I am.

✻

Oh, how much fun we have had over the years.
So much love, laughter and many memories.

✻

Thank you for being there through times of laughter, smiling, crying and sighing ... Looking forward to many more happy times together.

✻

A friendship like ours is as rare as diamonds.

✻

You are always there with your pearls of wisdom ... Thank you.

✻

I know you're a true friend because you tell me how it is—everyone else tells me what I want to hear. Thanks for keeping it honest.

Trouble? Us? Never!

*

Thank you for sharing your strength with me over this difficult time.

*

You make my world a happier place.

*

I feel blessed to have you as a friend. There is no need for pretence—
you allow me to be just as I am.

*

Thanks for being there in the good and the bad times.
Your friendship means the world to me.

*

May the sun never set on our friendship.

*

You have helped my dreams come true ... I hope I can do
the same for you.

*

To my partner in crime ... Thanks for all the fun we have had.

*

To my cool, smart, happy-go-lucky, beautiful friend ... I just had to let
you know how much our friendship means to me. I love you.

*

Dear (name) ... Thanks for always sharing.

*

Our friendship ... magic!

*

A friend is a companion of affection and esteem.
Thank you for being mine.

To my fellow life traveller ... let's stick to the same path.

✻

Our friendship is irreplaceable.

✻

To my soul sister, may our exceptional friendship
last from here to eternity.

✻

You are the only one who understands me when I make no sense at
all.

✻

Even though we are far apart, I don't know what I would do
without our conversations. Let's talk again soon.

✻

Even though life is busy just now, I am still thinking of you
and the value of our friendship.

✻

Our friendship is more beautiful to me than a bouquet of roses.

✻

Your friendship has been a ray of sunshine in my life.

✻

You have made all the difference in my life.

✻

I can live without a lot of things ... You're not one of them.

✻

You are my greatest friend, the one I can share my true feelings with.
Thank you.

✻

Every day is brighter from knowing you. You are a true friend.

Times may not always be smooth sailing between us, but when it counts you always come through for me. You are a true friend.

✳

You are reliable, dependable, faithful and loving even when I'm not. Thanks for being my friend.

✳

You always know how to make me laugh and look at the brighter side of life. Thanks for keeping me in good spirits.

✳

I know we will be friends forever.

✳

I am so grateful for you and the role you play in my life. You have been there through thick and thin and I will never take you for granted.

✳

You are the sunshine of my life. My days are so much brighter because of you.

✳

To my dearest friend. You make me so blooming happy.

✳

The gift of friendship is the most precious gift of all. Thank you for being so generous.

✳

Thank you for loving and accepting me just as I am. I am so glad I can call you my friend.

✳

Thank you for all the happiness you have brought into my life since we have been friends.

✳

You always have the best ideas for the most fun. I don't think I laughed half as much before I knew you.

You are irreplaceable, I could never find a better friend than you. You have helped me through all the hard times and we have celebrated together through the good. Thank you for our enduring friendship.

✻

To my most treasured friend. You are more valuable to me than the most precious stones. Thank you for being in my life, I would not trade you for anything.

✻

We have been friends for so long and I have loved sharing everything with you, the highs and lows and all we have achieved together and as individuals. I am looking forward to many more years of sharing ahead.

✻

I could not imagine that friendship could get any better than what we share. You have been the best friend that any person could be and I hope you know how much that means to me.

✻

You have supported me in everything I have wanted to do.
You have helped me make my dreams come true.
Thank you for believing in me, but more than that
thank you for being my friend.

✻

There is no special reason for this card. Other than to say that you are so special to me.

✻

When I think about all the people that mean so much to me I always think of you first.

✻

I am surer of myself because of our friendship. I know you will back me in anything I set out to do.

✻

I love that we can talk about everything and nothing at all.

Thank you for your strength and wisdom. I hope I can do the same for you. I cannot express to you how much I value our friendship.

✻

What are friends for? They are for sharing everything with.
Thank you for being my friend.

✻

You make me laugh until it hurts. I love you.

✻

I really needed you the other day. Only you could pull me out of the dumps like that. Thanks for being there.

✻

I love the times that we share a coffee and remember when...

✻

I love the way our conversations flow so easily, the way we laugh and cry. I love every minute we spend together and on the phone. But most of all I love you.

✻

I will always be grateful for the closeness we share. No one will ever be able to wedge their way or will between us.

✻

To my evil twin... who do you think is the bad influence in our relationship? Let's always paint the town red.

✻

To my friend and confidante, it has been so great to know that what we share is safer than any high security bank vault.
Thanks for everything.

✻

Only you understand my thoughts and feelings without me having to say a word. You always know exactly what to say and do. I cannot imagine never having found a friend like you.

I know I will always have some place to go. Thank you for always being there for me.

✳

I am so happy to share the journey of life with you by my side. Our friendship means so much to me and with you in my life I know that we can get through anything.

✳

Thank you for your honesty and truth. Thank you for dropping everything to be with me in my time of need. Thank you for just being you!

✳

My life could not be any better, simply because I have a friend named [name].

✳

You know how prone I am to making mistakes, but having you as a friend is so right. I know I could never make the mistake of losing you.

✳

*'A real friend is one who walks in
when the rest of the world walks out.'*
Walter Winchell (1897–1972), US journalist and author

✳

*'In prosperity our friends know us;
in adversity we know our friends.'*
John Churton Collins (1848–1908), English literary critic

✳

'A friend is one who sees through you and still enjoys the view.'
Wilma Askinas (1926–), US author and columnist

✳

Friends are the family we choose ourselves.   Unknown

✳

Life is partly what we make it, and partly what it is made by the friends we choose. Tennessee Williams

You meet people who forget you. You forget people you meet. But sometimes you meet those people you can't forget. Those are your friends. Unknown

✳

Real friends are those who, when you feel you've made a fool of yourself, don't feel you've done a permanent job. Unknown

✳

Friendship is always a sweet responsibility, never an opportunity.
Kahlil Gibran

✳

True friendship isn't about being there when it's convenient; it's about being there when it's not. Unknown

✳

A friend is someone who knows the song in your heart and can sing it back to you when you have forgotten the words. Unknown

✳

Friends are the pillars on your porch. Sometimes they hold you up, sometimes they lean on you, and sometimes it's just enough to know that they are standing by. Unknown

✳

Celebrate the happiness that friends are always giving, Make every day a holiday and celebrate just living!
Amanda Bradley

✳

The most beautiful discovery true friends make is that they can grow separately without growing apart. Elisabeth Foley

✳

Only your real friends tell you when your face is dirty.
Sicilian proverb

✳

Your secrets are safe with me and all my friends. Unknown

I get by with a little help from my friends. John Lennon

✻

A true friend is someone who thinks that you are a good egg even though he knows that you are slightly cracked. Bernard Meltzer

✻

*I can no other answer make,
but, thanks, and thanks.*
William Shakespeare

✻

*The smallest act of kindness is worth more
than the grandest intention.* Oscar Wilde

✻

How beautiful a day can be when kindness touches it!
George Elliston

✻

*What we have done for ourselves alone dies with us; what we
have done for others and the world remains and is immortal.*
Albert Pike

✻

*Kindness is the language which the deaf can hear
and the blind can see.* Mark Twain

✻

*The only people with whom you should try to get even are those
who have helped you.* John E Southard

✻

*One can pay back the loan of gold, but one lies forever
in debt to those who are kind.* Malayan proverb

✻

*Unselfish and noble actions are the most radiant pages in the
biography of souls.* David Thomas

It's nice to be important, but it's more important to be nice.
Unknown

✳

I feel a very unusual sensation—if it is not indigestion, I think it must be gratitude. Benjamin Disraeli

✳

I would maintain that thanks are the highest form of thought, and that gratitude is happiness doubled by wonder.
G K Chesterton

✳

Not what we give,
But what we share,
For the gift
without the giver
is bare.
James Russell Lowell

✳

How far that little candle throws his beams!
So shines a good deed in a weary world.
William Shakespeare

✳

Your secrets are safe with me and all my friends. Unknown

✳

A friend may well be reckoned a masterpiece of nature. Unknown

✳

It is chance that made us co-workers [or any word] but hearts that made us friends. Unknown

✳

Friends are the flowers in life's garden. Unknown

✳

A friend is one who believes in you when you have ceased to believe in yourself. Unknown

Love is blind, but friendship closes its eyes. Unknown

✳

A friend's house is never far. Unknown

✳

What is a friend? I will tell you it is someone with whom you dare to be yourself. Frank Crane

✳

Friendship is the wine of life. Unknown

✳

A friend is someone who understands your past, believes in your future and accepts you just the way you are. Unknown

✳

A true friend is someone who reaches for your hand and touches your heart. Unknown

Thank You

Thanks [name] for everything you do, but mostly just for being you!

✳

Thank you for giving up your precious time to be involved in mine. You are more than a friend—you are a friend that cares! Thanks again!

✳

You couldn't be nicer, I couldn't be happier,
and words couldn't thank you enough!

✳

With lives as busy as ours, we often forget the most
important people in them—so it's way past time I said
a very belated thank you for your kindness!

✳

Thanks for all the things you do and the really nice way you do them!

✳

Thank you for supporting me in my time of need.

✳

Thank you ... You made my day.

✳

Thank you. You are the key that opens doors.

✳

I am touched by all you have done ... Thank you.

✳

Thank you for all the little things you do. It means the world to me.

✳

It only takes one person's random act of kindness to make a difference.
Thank you for making a difference in my life.

✳

Many thanks. May your kindness be returned to you a hundredfold.

You made what was a difficult situation much easier to bear.
Thank you.

✻

Thank you for helping me get through a tough time, for your shoulder
to cry on and for listening to me blabber on and on.

✻

Your generosity and kind heart will never be forgotten. Thank you.

✻

Thank you for your grace in this situation. You are a beautiful person.

✻

While others talked, you acted. Thank you.

✻

You have moved my heart. Thank you.

✻

Thank you for giving up your precious time and energy
to make my load easier.

✻

I am touched by your love. Thank you.

✻

Thank you for being there when I needed you most.

✻

Your thoughtfulness has made such a difference in my life.

✻

Your act of kindness has touched me more than you know. Thank you.

✻

I clearly have impeccable taste in friends ... Thank you.

✻

Your thoughtfulness and kindness made my day... Thank you

You always go the extra mile... Thank you

✳

I am always overwhelmed by your kindness and generosity.
My life would be darkness without your light.

✳

Thankyou for taking the time to remember me at this time

✳

Thank you for always being so dependable, trustworthy and reliable.
You are one of the greatest treasures in my life

✳

Your thoughtfulness knows no limits. Just as my appreciation has no
bounds.

✳

I am speechless with appreciation. Without your support and kindness
I don't know how I would have found the strength to go on.

✳

You are such a credit to the people around you and I just wanted to
take this moment to recognise all you have done.

✳

It was so wonderful to have you join us on our special day. It was such
a blessing to have you surrounding us with your love.

✳

It is people like you who make this world a better place. Thank you for
being in our lives.

✳

Your thoughtfulness is extraordinary. Your special touch and knowing
just what to say makes me so thankful that you are my friend.

✳

To a true friend who is just as beautiful on the inside as she is on the
outside. Thank you for all your help at this time.

You have truly proved that actions speak so much louder than words.
Thanks for all your help.

✳

Your simple acts of kindness show that you really care.
Thank you for being my friend.

✳

Please accept this as a token of my appreciation for all you have done.

✳

I am forever in your debt. I hope you can count on me the way I can
count on you. Thank you for everything.

✳

*I would thank you from the bottom of my heart, but for you my
heart has no bottom.* Unknown

✳

I can no other answer make, but, thanks, and thanks. William
Shakespeare

✳

*Blessed are those that can give without remembering and receive
without forgetting.* Unknown

✳

*We can only be said to be alive in those moments when our hearts
are conscious of our treasures.* Thornton Wilder

✳

*If the only prayer you ever say in your entire life is thank you, it
will be enough.* Meister Eckhardt

✳

*Let us be grateful to people who make us happy; they are the
charming gardeners who make our souls blossom.* Marcel Proust

CONGRATULATIONS

Congratulations on your success. It is a
reflection of your strength and character.

✳

Congratulations. We are celebrating with you.

New Home

Congratulations on your new home.
May it be filled with love and joy.

✳

May joy and peace be yours in your new home.

✳

Congratulations on your new home. May it be a
special place for friends, family and memories.

✳

May every day in your new home create memories that
will be cherished forever.

✳

May God bless your new house as you make it a home.

✳

May the time shared together in your new home be full of love and
laughter.

✳

Congratulations on your new home. We're looking forward
to spending time with you there.

✳

It's the people in the house that make it a home, so we know
yours will be a beautiful one.

✳

There is no place like home. Except maybe the mall... it feels like home
to me. Congratulations on your new place.

May your new home be a haven where you and your family make wonderful memories.

✻

Any place you are is home to me so I know this one will be just as special. Congratulations.

✻

It won't be long before your new house becomes a home and haven.

✻

Home is where your junk is.

✻

Its not every day you move house (that's a relief). May you have years of happiness and prosperity in your new home.

✻

As you move into your new home, may good times and fond memories move with you.

✻

Looking forward to spending time with you in your new home and making special memories there.

✻

Home, the spot of earth supremely blest,
A dearer, sweeter spot than all the rest.
Robert Montgomery

✻

May your home always be too small to hold
all of your friends.   Unknown

✻

I am grateful for the lawn that needs mowing, windows that need
cleaning, and floors that need waxing because it means
I have a home.   Unknown

May your walls know joy;
May every room hold laughter
And every window open to
Great possibility.
Unknown

✳

It takes hands to build a house, but only hearts can build a home.
Unknown

✳

Where we love is home—home that our feet may leave,
but not our hearts.   Oliver Wendell Holmes, Sr

✳

Every house where love abides
And friendship is a guest,
Is surely home, and home sweet home
For there the heart can rest.
Henry Van Dyke

✳

The ornaments of your house will be the guests who frequent it.
Unknown

✳

The fellow that owns his own home is always just coming out
of a hardware store.   Frank McKinney Hubbard

Graduation

Congratulations on making it to the end.

✳

We are so proud of you. We are looking forward
to seeing your prosperous future unfold.

We are so proud of you and trust that wherever the road leads or whatever turn you decide to make it will be the right one.

✳

Best wishes for the future ... wherever it leads.
Congratulations on a huge milestone. Wishing you
lots of happiness on your graduation.

✳

You have done your best. Be proud of all you have accomplished.

✳

Congratulations ... it's time to make your mark on the world.

✳

Wishing you joy and so much more on your graduation.

✳

Congratulations. Reach for the stars.

✳

We are proud of you (name) ... Your commitment and enthusiasm have
been inspiring ... Well done.

✳

When we finish something, it's followed by a new beginning.
I'm looking forward to hearing all about yours.

✳

Well done. You've worked hard and deserve a successful
and promising future.

✳

Today is the promise of a very bright future. Congratulations.

✳

The world is full of exciting possibilities and they have just been
opened up to you. Have fun exploring them.

✳

Con 'grad' ulations!

I still remember when you took your first tentative steps in the world of [high school/college/uni] and here you are now running to your future. Congratulations.

✳

Change is inevitable, except from that dodgy vending machine in the cafeteria. Good luck in your future endeavours.

✳

May the memories from the past years always bring you a smile as you now step forward into a new chapter.

✳

May the dreams you've had in the past become the reality of your future.

✳

As you step out into a new adventure, hold on to your values; don't let yourself become jaded. Achieve all that you have prepared yourself for. Congratulations.

✳

Not only is this day a remarkable occasion, but you are a remarkable person.

✳

The future belongs to those who believe in the beauty of their dreams. Eleanor Roosevelt

✳

Put your future in good hands—your own. Unknown

✳

You have brains in your head.
You have feet in your shoes.
You can steer yourself any direction you choose. Dr. Seuss

✳

It is the mark of an educated mind to be able to entertain a thought without accepting it. Aristotle

✳

Your schooling may be over, but remember that your education still continues. Unknown

✳

Go confidently in the direction of your dreams. Live the life you have imagined. Henry David Thoreau

✳

When you leave here, don't forget why you came.
Adlai Stevenson, to college graduates

✳

Don't live down to expectations. Go out there and do something remarkable. Wendy Wasserstein

✳

All successful people, men and women, are big dreamers. They imagine what their future could be, ideal in every respect, and then they work every day towards their distant vision, that goal or purpose. Brian Tracy

✳

I hope your dreams take you to the corners of your smiles, to the highest of your hopes, to the windows of your opportunities, and to the most special places your heart has ever known. Unknown

✳

Don't judge each day by the harvest you reap but by the seeds that you plant. Robert Louis Stevenson

✳

You cannot help but learn more as you take the world into your hands. Take it up reverently, for it is an old piece of clay, with millions of thumbprints on it.
John Updike

✳

Hitch your wagon to a star. Ralph Waldo Emerson

Do not follow where the path may lead.
Go instead where there is no path and leave a trail.
Harold R. McAlindon

If you can imagine it, you can achieve it; if you can dream it, you can become it. William Arthur Ward

＊

The horizon leans forward, offering you space to place new steps of change. Maya Angelou

＊

Think big thoughts but relish small pleasures.
H. Jackson Brown

＊

You are educated. Your certification is in your degree. You may think of it as the ticket to the good life. Let me ask you to think of an alternative. Think of it as your ticket to change the world.
Tom Brokaw

＊

Your families are extremely proud of you. You can't imagine the sense of relief they are experiencing. This would be a most opportune time to ask for money. Gary Bolding

＊

The important thing is not to stop questioning. Albert Einstein

＊

An investment in knowledge always pays the best interest.
Benjamin Franklin

＊

A graduation ceremony is an event where the commencement speaker tells thousands of students dressed in identical caps and gowns that 'individuality' is the key to success. Robert Orben

The man who graduates today and stops learning tomorrow is uneducated the day after. Newton D Baker

✳

At commencement you wear your square-shaped mortarboards. My hope is that from time to time you will let your minds be bold, and wear sombreros. Paul Freund

Promotion

Congratulations on your promotion.
I can't think of a more deserving person.

✳

Congratulations on your promotion. You deserve it.

✳

For someone who works as hard as you, it was only
a matter of time. Well done.

✳

We knew they would see your potential eventually.

✳

It couldn't have happened to a better person. Congratulations.

✳

A well-earned promotion. Congratulations, you deserve it.

✳

Keep on moving up... Congratulations on your promotion.
There was never any doubt your effort would pay off. Congratulations
on your new role.

✳

You have cracked it. Welcome to a whole new level of hard work.

✳

You are destined for greatness. Enjoy this new journey and the places
it takes you.

You are where you are supposed to be. Congratulations.

*

Without promotion something terrible happens... Nothing!
P. T. Barnum

*

Enthusiasm is the engine of success. Ralph Waldo Emerson

*

*I've got a theory that if you give 100 percent all of the time,
somehow things will work out in the end.* Larry Bird

*

*Being ready isn't enough; you have to be prepared for a promotion
or any other significant change.* Pat Riley

*

*I'm a great believer in luck, and I find the harder I work the more I
have of it.* Thomas Jefferson

*

*Accomplishing the impossible means only that the boss
will add it to your regular duties.* Doug Larson

*

*By working faithfully eight hours a day you may eventually get to
be boss and work twelve hours a day.* Robert Frost

*Executive ability is deciding quickly and getting somebody else
to do the work.* John G Pollard

*

*I cannot put into words just how much promotion means to me
but if I could I would put it in a can so I could open it later.*
Steve Coppell

Congratulations. May this job be everything you hoped it would be.

*

Congratulations. You'll do great.

*

Hoping your new job is so great you won't be able to stop smiling.

*

Enjoy the journey and remember to have fun.

*

Congrats. Hoping this new job is the beginning of
an even better future.

*

No more sleeping in and long lazy breakfasts for you. Welcome to the
real world. Congratulations, you will love it!

*

So here you are facing the first day in your new career. Embrace your
future and you will succeed.

*

[I/We] know you will go far. You always give 110%.

*

Your enthusiasm, loyalty and commitment are assurance that you will
go far in your new job. All the best for the future.

*

A new job brings with it so many new experiences and opportunities.
Enjoy the ride!

*

Another success and I am sure there will be many more.
Congratulations on your new job.

*

The closest to perfection a person ever comes is when he fills out a job application form. Stanley J. Randall

✳

Researchers at Harvard say that taking a power nap for an hour in the afternoon can totally refresh you. They say that by the time you wake up you'll feel so good, you'll be able to start looking for a new job. Jay Leno

Pleasure in the job puts perfection in the work. Aristotle

✳

Whenever you are asked if you can do a job, tell 'em, "Certainly, I can!" Then get busy and find out how to do it. Theodore Roosevelt

✳

Home is the place where, when you have to go there,
They have to take you in.
Robert Frost, *The Death of the Hired Man*

✳

The light is what guides you home, the warmth is what keeps you there. Ellie Rodriguez

✳

There is nothing like staying at home for real comfort. Jane Austen

✳

Home is a place you grow up wanting to leave, and grow old wanting to get back to. John Ed Pearce

✳

Home is a shelter from storms—all sorts of storms. William J. Bennett

✳

A house is made of walls and beams; a home is built with love and dreams. William Arthur Ward

✳

Find a job you like and you add five days to every week.
H Jackson Browne

The best way to appreciate your job is to imagine yourself without one. Oscar Wilde

✳

Choose a job you love, and you will never have to work a day in your life. Confucius

Don't waste time learning the 'tricks of the trade'. Instead, learn the trade. Attributed to both James Charlton and H Jackson Brown

✳

The brain is a wonderful organ. It starts working the moment you get up in the morning, and does not stop until you get into the office. Robert Frost

✳

If you have a job without any aggravations, you don't have a job. Malcolm S Forbes

✳

The supreme accomplishment is to blur the line between work and play. Arnold Toynbee

✳

Many people quit looking for work when they find a job. Unknown

✳

The difference between a job and a career is the difference between forty and sixty hours a week. Robert Frost

✳

When people go to work, they shouldn't have to leave their hearts at home. Betty Bender

✳

A lot of fellows nowadays have a B.A., M.D., or Ph.D. Unfortunately, they don't have a J.O.B. 'Fats' Domino

Time is an illusion, lunchtime doubly so.   Douglas Adams

✽

*Whenever it is possible, a boy should choose some occupation
which he should do even if he did not need the money.*
William Lyon Phelps

New Business

A business that makes nothing but money is a poor business.
Henry Ford

✽

All the best with your new business venture.
We know it will be very successful.

✽

You have always succeeded in everything you do.
We know this will be no different ... All the best.

✽

With your enthusiasm and commitment, your new business is
guaranteed to succeed.

✽

Good luck with your new adventure. Not that someone as thoughtful and
astute as you would ever need luck!

✽

With your pioneering spirit, careful consideration and unwavering
integrity you will go far. I look forward to hearing
of your success.

✽

I applaud your courage and sense of adventure. Good luck, I have no
doubt you will go far.

✽

I was so excited to hear of your pioneering venture. I am sure you will
achieve much success.

Opportunity has knocked and you have opened the door. Embrace your future and you will succeed.

✳

Nothing ventured nothing gained. [I/We] know you are going to be a huge success.

✳

The absolute fundamental aim is to make money out of satisfying customers. John Egan

✳

Life is either a daring adventure or nothing. Helen Keller

✳

The man who will use his skill and constructive imagination to see how much he can give for a dollar, instead of how little he can give for a dollar, is bound to succeed. Henry Ford

✳

A business that makes nothing but money is a poor business. Henry Ford

✳

In the business world, everyone is paid in two coins: cash and experience. Take the experience first; the cash will come later. Harold Geneen

✳

To be successful, you have to have your heart in your business, and your business in your heart. Thomas Watson, Sr.

✳

They can because they think they can. Virgil

✳

Success is the sum of small efforts, repeated day in and day out. Robert Collier

✳

Keep steadily before you the fact that all true success depends at last upon yourself. Theodore T. Hunger

*

Wise are those who learn that the bottom line doesn't always have to be their top priority. William Arthur Ward

*

Your most unhappy customers are your greatest source of learning. Bill Gates, *Business @ the Speed of Thought*

*

The sign on the door of opportunity reads PUSH.   Unknown

*

I'm not a driven businessman, but a driven artist. I never think about money. Beautiful things make money.   Lord Acton

*

When in doubt, mumble; when in trouble, delegate; when in charge, ponder.   James H Boren

*

The secret to productive goal setting is in establishing clearly defined goals, writing them down and then focusing on them several times a day with words, pictures and emotions as if we've already achieved them.   Denis Waitley

*

Most of what we call management consists of making it difficult for people to get their work done.   Peter Drucker

*

As a small businessperson, you have no greater leverage than the truth.   John Greenleaf Whittier

*

In the business world, everyone is paid in two coins: cash and experience. Take the experience first; the cash will come later.
Harold S Geneen

The secret to managing is to keep the guys who hate you away from the guys who are undecided. Casey Stengel

✱

And while the law of competition may be sometimes hard for the individual, it is best for the race, because it ensures the survival of the fittest in every department. Andrew Carnegie

✱

I rate enthusiasm even above professional skill. Edward Appleton

✱

High achievement always takes place in the framework of high expectation. Charles Kettering

✱

Do more than is required. What is the distance between someone who achieves their goals consistently and those who spend their lives and careers merely following? The extra mile. Gary Ryan Blair

✱

Every young man would do well to remember that all successful business stands on the foundation of morality.
Henry Ward Beecher

✱

Remind people that profit is the difference between revenue and expense. This makes you look smart. Scott Adams

QUOTES

'When you've got it, flaunt it!'
Zero Mostel, in the film *The Producers*

*

'Winning is not everything. It's the only thing.'
Vince Lombardi (1913–1970), US pro football coach

*

'The happiest people in life don't have the best of everything ...
they make the best of everything they have.
Congratulations on doing the best of all!' Unknown

Christmas

Peace and joy at Christmas and throughout the New Year.

*

Wishing you a Merry Christmas and a prosperous New Year.

*

Merry Christmas and thank you for your friendship throughout the year.

*

May love and joy be yours this Christmas time and into the New Year.

*

Glory to God in the highest, and on Earth peace to all men.

*

Joy to the world—and especially to you.

*

This card brings love and wishes at Christmas time just for you.

*

The season of peace, joy and sharing is here again.
To you and your family we send our love and best wishes.

*

May your New Year be filled with health and prosperity.

*

At this special time of year, warm wishes of love and peace
I send to you.

*

Christmas is a special time to remember all those valuable times together.

*

May your Christmas day be blessed with an
abundance of joy, peace and compassion.

*

When I think of you, it's Christmas every day.

*

You are the decoration of my life. Merry Christmas!

*

From our home to yours, we send love
and best wishes at this Christmas time.

*

It only takes ONE good friend to brighten the whole season!
Merry Christmas!

*

In the spirit of the season, may your holiday be filled with
joy, love and laughter. Merry Christmas.

*

Abundant good wishes for happiness and joy this holiday season.

*

May your treasures this Christmas be a home full of laughter,
memories
and happiness, friendships rekindled and hearts filled with joy.

*

Christmas is a time for eating, laughing, caring, sharing, giving
and receiving. I hope you experience all of them.

*

May your home be filled with love, laughter and Christmas spirit.

*

Wishing you joy on this special season of miraculous wonder.

*

May your Christmas be bright with, love, joy and light.
From our family to yours ... Merry Christmas.

*

May the beauty of this season fill your heart and home with joy ...
Merry Christmas.

May you look back on this wonderful Christmas season throughout the year with fond memories of fun times.

✻

May the peace of God be with you and your family this holiday season and may He keep you safe from harm ... All our love the (name) Family.

✻

Although the weather is warm, may you be snowed under with love, joy and peace this Christmas.

✻

May your Christmas be a blessed one with family and friends.

✻

A silent night with a bright shining star ... May this Christmas fill you with peace, hope, and joy to sustain you through the New Year.

✻

May each day of this holiday season be full of love, friendship and peace ... Merry Christmas.

✻

As we celebrate the birth of Jesus, I pray this Christmas brings you joy.

✻

Wishing you a beautiful Christmas season with time for relaxation and contemplation.

✻

It's a busy time of year, make sure you find time to stop and enjoy.

✻

As you awake on Christmas morn, lie still a moment and enjoy a moment's peace before the onslaught of children and wrapping paper. May the spirit of Christmas fill your homes this holiday season.

✻

Peace, love and prosperity from our family to yours.

✻

May this Christmas time with family friends renew your spirit for the
new year.

✳

May you experience all the joys of this holiday season
to the fullest.

✳

Christmas is that magical season where families and friends come
together to celebrate the birth of the saviour. Merry Christmas to you
and your family.

✳

During this crazy time of year, make sure you take the time to stop
and enjoy the beauty of the season.

✳

The best of love the best of cheer for you and your family, both now
and into the New Year.

✳

May fun and happy times decorate your life this Christmas.

✳

'Tis the season to be jolly.
Let your hair down and have a good time.

✳

From home to home and heart to heart, may the joy of Christmas
travel from our family to yours. Merry Christmas.

✳

Even though we are far apart, the warmth and joy of Christmas draws
us closer to each other.

✳

May the wonder of the season travel with you into the New Year and
beyond.

✳

My gift to you this year is all my love wrapped up in the tightest hug. Lots of love to you and your family this Christmas.

*

Lights, trees, mistletoe and gifts... may you enjoy all of these, but most of all the gift of God's son.

*

May the gifts of love, hope and charity be yours this holiday season.

'At Christmas play and make good cheer,
For Christmas comes but once a year.'
Thomas Tusser (c. 1515–80), English author

✳

'And is it true?
And is it true,
This most tremendous tale of all,
Seen in a stained-glass window's hue,
A Baby in an ox's stall?
The Maker of the stars and sea,
Became a Child on earth for me?'
Sir John Betjeman (1906–84), British poet

✳

'I heard the bells on Christmas Day
Their old familiar carols play,
And wild and sweet the words repeat
Of peace on Earth, good will to men!'
Henry Wadsworth Longfellow (1807–82), US poet

✳

'The feet of the humblest may walk in the field
Where the feet of the holiest trod,
This, then, is the marvel to mortals revealed.'
Phillips Brooks (1835–93), US Episcopal bishop

✳

'Good news from heaven the angels bring,
Glad tidings to the earth they sing:
To us this day a child is given,
To crown us with the joy of heaven.'
Martin Luther (1483–1586), German Protestant theologian

'Somehow, not only for Christmas
But all the long year through,
The joy that you give to others
Is the joy that comes back to you.
And the more you spend in blessing
The poor and lonely and sad,
The more of your heart's possessing
Returns to you glad.'
John Greenleaf Whittier (1807–92), US poet

✳

'I will honor Christmas in my heart, and try to keep it all the year.'
Charles Dickens (1812–70), English novelist

✳

'Then ye be glad, good people,
This night of all the year,
And light ye up your candles:
His star is shining near.'
Unknown

✳

'Love came down at Christmas,
Love all lovely, love divine;
Love was born at Christmas;
Star and angels gave the sign.'
Christina Georgina Rossetti (1830–94), British poet

✳

'And she will bear a son, and you shall call his name Jesus,
for it is he who will save his people from their sins.'
Matthew 1:21

'Now when Jesus was born in Bethlehem of Judea in the days of
Herod the king, behold, there came wise men from the east to
Jerusalem, saying, where is he that is born King of the Jews? For
we have seen his star in the east, and are come to worship him.'
Matthew 2:1–2

✳

'Happy, happy Christmas, that can win us back to the delusions of our childhood days, recall to the old man the pleasures of his youth, and transport the traveller back to his own fireside and quiet home!'
Charles Dickens (1812–70), English novelist

✳

'Blessed is the season which engages the whole world in a conspiracy of love.'
Hamilton Wright Mabie (1845–1916), US author

✳

'What is Christmas? It is tenderness for the past, courage for the present, hope for the future. It is a fervent wish that every cup may overflow with blessings rich and eternal, and that every path may lead to peace.' Agnes M. Pharo, unknown

✳

'The joy of brightening other lives, bearing each others' burdens, easing other's loads and supplanting empty hearts and lives with generous gifts becomes for us the magic of Christmas.'
W.C. Jones

✳

'Whatever else be lost among the years,
Let us keep Christmas still a shining thing:
Whatever doubts assail us, or what fears,
Let us hold close one day, remembering
Its poignant meaning for the hearts of men.
Let us get back our childlike faith again.'
Grace Noll Crowell (1877–1969), US poet

✳

I will honour Christmas in my heart,
and try to keep it all the year.
Charles Dickens

✳

Your Merry Christmas may depend on what others do for you ...
but your Happy New Year depends on what you do for others.
Unknown

Love is what's in the room with you at Christmas if you stop opening presents and listen. Unknown

✻

Remember, if Christmas isn't found in your heart, you won't find it under a tree. Charlotte Carpenter

✻

Sugar and Spice makes Christmas Nice! Unknown

✻

Three wonderful little words at Christmas ... No Assembly Required! Unknown

✻

One of the most glorious messes in the world is the mess created in the living room on Christmas day. Don't clean it up too quickly. Andy Rooney

✻

A little smile, a word of cheer,
A bit of love from someone near,
A little gift from one held dear,
Best wishes for the coming year ...
These make a Merry Christmas!
John Greenleaf Whittier

✻

Peace on earth will come to stay,
when we live Christmas every day. Helen Steiner Rice

✻

Christmas cookies and happy hearts, this is how the holiday starts.
Unknown

✻

Perhaps the best Yuletide decoration is being wreathed in smiles.
Unknown

✻

Christmas waves a magic wand over this world, and behold, everything is softer and more beautiful. Norman Vincent Peale

✳

Bless us Lord, this Christmas, with quietness of mind; Teach us to be patient and always to be kind. Helen Steiner Rice

✳

It is Christmas in the heart that puts Christmas in the air. W T Ellis

✳

For centuries men have kept an appointment with Christmas. Christmas means fellowship, feasting, giving and receiving, a time of good cheer, home. W J Tucker

✳

Christmas is forever, not for just one day, for loving, sharing, giving, are not to put away like bells and lights and tinsel, in some box upon a shelf. The good you do for others is good you do yourself. Norman W Brooks, *Let Every Day Be Christmas*

✳

At Christmas, all roads lead home. Marjorie Holmes

✳

Gifts of time and love are surely the basic ingredients for a truly Merry Christmas. Peg Bracken

✳

Every time we love, every time we give, it's Christmas. Dale Evans

✳

There's nothing sadder in this world than to awake Christmas morning and not be a child. Erma Bombeck

✳

From a commercial point of view, if Christmas did not exist it would be necessary to invent it. Katherine Whitehorn in her book *Roundabout*

Christmas is not a time nor a season, but a state of mind. To cherish peace and goodwill, to be plenteous in mercy, is to have the real spirit of Christmas. Calvin Coolidge

*

I wish we could put some of the Christmas spirit in jars and open a jar of it every month.
Harlan Miller

*

Christmas gift suggestions:
To your enemy, forgiveness.
To an opponent, tolerance.
To a friend, your heart.
To a customer, service.
To all, charity.
To every child, a good example.
To yourself, respect.
Oren Arnold

*

"Glory to God in the highest, and on earth peace, goodwill toward men." Luke 2:14

*

Christmas, children, is not a date.
It is a state of mind. Mary Ellen Chase

*

I will honour Christmas in my heart, and try to keep it all the year.
Charles Dickens

From home to home, and heart to heart, from one place to another. The warmth and joy of Christmas, brings us closer to each other. Emily Matthews

*

Never worry about the size of your Christmas tree. In the eyes of children, they are all 30 feet tall. Larry Wilde

*

Christmas is doing a little something extra for someone. Unknown

✳

Peace on earth will come to stay,
When we live Christmas every day. Helen Steiner Rice

✳

Christmas is the season for kindling the fire of hospitality in the
hall, the genial flame of charity in the heart. Washington Irving

✳

The best of all gifts around any Christmas tree: the presence of a
happy family all wrapped up in each other. Burton Hillis

✳

Christmas: that magic blanket that wraps itself about us, that
something so intangible that it is like a fragrance. It may weave a
spell of nostalgia. Christmas may be a day of feasting, or of prayer,
but always it will be a day of remembrance—a day in which we
think of everything we have ever loved. Augusta E. Rundel

✳

Christmas is the gentlest, loveliest festival of the revolving year—
and yet, for all that, when it speaks, its voice has strong authority.
W. J. Cameron

✳

Christmas is most truly Christmas when we celebrate it by giving
the light of love to those who need it most.
Ruth Carter Stapleton

✳

Christmas Eve was a night of song that wrapped itself about you
like a shawl. But it warmed more than your body. It warmed your
heart... filled it, too, with a melody that would last forever.
Bess Streeter Aldrich

✳

Christmas, my child, is love in action. Every time we love, every
time we give, it's Christmas. Dale Evans Rogers

✳

Christmas! The very word brings joy to our hearts. No matter how we may dread the rush, the long Christmas lists for gifts and cards to be bought and given—when Christmas Day comes there is still the same warm feeling we had as children, the same warmth that enfolds our hearts and our homes. Joan Winmill Brown

*

Santa is very jolly because he knows where all the bad girls live.
Unknown

Easter

Rejoice in the Lord! May all the beauty and glory of this blessed season fill our hearts with praise. Happy Easter.

✳

Shout for joy, all the earth, lift up your voice and sing! Christ the Lord is risen today. He reigns on high as King! Wishing you a joyful, meaningful Easter.

✳

Alleluia! Christ is risen! Sharing with you the miracles of new hope and new life. Have a joyous Easter.

✳

An Easter wish—May the glory of our living Lord renew your hopes, your faith, your joy. Have a blessed Easter season.

✳

An Easter wish—On this day, may you experience a sweet renewal of faith, hope, and joy.

✳

Easter greetings. Warmest wishes for a season of sweet discoveries.

✳

Easter is a time of remembrance. I will not forget you! Happy Easter.

✳

Thinking of you at Easter. Wishing you and those you love the blessings of a glorious Easter.

✳

This special prayer at Easter-time is coming to convey, the hope that all God's love and grace will light your Easter day! Easter is a time of reflection and joy, when we emerge from our cocoon of doubt to fly freely on the wings of faith. May you be renewed and strengthened in the promise of our Lord.

✳

For you—a wish for the happiest of Easters.

Remember, no matter how mature and sophisticated
you may become, you never outgrow
your need for chocolate bunnies! Happy Easter.

✳

There's no time like Easter for remembering just how wonderful
God's love really is. Blessings to you and yours.

✳

For you at Easter—May the joy of Christ's resurrection
live in your heart today and always.

✳

Wishing you and those you love a joyous celebration of renewed faith.
Have a blessed Easter.

✳

Easter celebrates God's gift of love: 'Neither height nor depth,
nor anything else in all creation, will be able to separate us
from the love of God.' (Romans 8:39) May you see his
mighty hand in every detail of your life. Happy Easter.

✳

Take time to contemplate the miracle of Easter and let this
fill your heart with warmth.

✳

Let your faith be renewed this Easter.

✳

Thinking of you and your family this Easter. May it be filled
with love laughter and above all ... chocolate.

✳

May your Easter be as warm and fuzzy as the bunny
who delivered your eggs!

✳

May your heart and home be filled with God's blessings this Easter.

As we celebrate this special season let's not forget
God's awesome gift ... Happy Easter.

*

Let us rejoice today as we remember the death and celebrate the
resurrection of our Lord Jesus Christ. Hallelujah.

*

Warm hot cross buns with melted butter, chocolate in every shape and
form ... mmm, smells like Easter! ... Have a great day.

*

As we come together at Easter, let's not forget the wonderful gift of
God's son.

*

May Christ's resurrection give your life meaning and direction no
matter what your circumstances.

*

May your faith be renewed this Easter as we contemplate this special
time.

*

New life, new day and new hope. Happy Easter.

*

Take time to stop and contemplate the miracle of Easter. Wishing you
and your family a wonderful weekend together.

*

Hoppy Easter from the Easter Bunny.

*

May this Easter be eggs-tra special.

*

May you and your family be blessed this Easter weekend.

*

May hope and love be forever part of your life because of what He has
done.

May the triumph of Jesus bless you with every good thing.
Happy Easter.

✳

I thank the Lord for our shared friendship and faith.
Happy Easter.

✳

As you enjoy all the treats of Easter take the time to mindfully
contemplate Jesus and all He has done.

Easter QUOTES

*Jesus took my place on the cross
to give me a place in heaven.* Unknown

✳

*The resurrection gives my life meaning and direction and the
opportunity to start over no matter what my circumstances.*
Robert Flatt

✳

*But from this earth, this grave, this dust,
My God shall raise me up, I trust.*
Walter Raleigh

✳

*Jesus lives, to Him the Throne
Over all the world is given,
May we go where He is gone,
Rest and reign with Him in heaven.
Alleluia!*
Christian Furchtegott Gellert

✳

Easter spells out beauty, the rare beauty of new life. S D Gordon

✳

*The cross of Christ shows us that God's love is of deepest descent
... universal distribution and of eternal duration.* Dr Fred Barlow

Let the resurrection joy lift us from loneliness and weakness and despair to strength and beauty and happiness. Floyd W Tomkins

✳

For I remember it is Easter morn,
And life and love and peace are all new born.
Alice Freeman Palmer

✳

Let every man and woman count himself immortal. Let him catch the revelation of Jesus in his resurrection. Let him say not merely, 'Christ is risen', but 'I shall rise'. Phillips Brooks

✳

Where man sees but withered leaves, God sees sweet flowers growing. Albert Laighton

✳

We live and die; Christ died and lived! John Stott

✳

All I really need is love, but a little chocolate now and then doesn't hurt! Lucy Van Pelt in *Peanuts* by Charles M. Schulz

✳

And he departed from our sight that we might return to our heart, and there find Him. For He departed, and behold, He is here. St. Augustine, *Confessions*

✳

Easter says you can put truth in a grave,
but it won't stay there. Clarence W. Hall

✳

Jesus took my place on the cross to give me a place in heaven.
Unknown

✳

Forget love—I'd rather fall in chocolate!!! Author unknown

"Christ the Lord is risen to-day,"
Sons of men and angels say.
Raise your joys and triumphs high;
Sing, ye heavens, and earth reply.
Charles Wesley, 'Christ the Lord is Risen To-Day'

Let the resurrection joy lift us from loneliness and weakness and despair to strength and beauty and happiness. Floyd W. Tomkins

Easter is the demonstration of God that life is essentially spiritual and timeless. Charles M. Crowe

Get Well

'He who has health has hope, but he who has hope has everything.'
—Arab proverb

Sorry you have not been well. Our thoughts and prayers
are with you for a speedy recovery.

✳

I feel bad that you feel bad—get well soon.

✳

Feelin' poorly? Well bless your heart—and every other little part!

✳

The doctor says you'll be back to normal soon—that'll be a first!
Get well soon!

✳

Looking forward to the return of your warm smile.

✳

We are praying you will be back to your wonderful self again
really soon.

Hoping each day brings you renewed strength, a brighter smile
and a happier you. Get well soon.

✳

Get well soon but not so quickly that you don't get to enjoy the
benefits of convalescing. Enjoy being cared for. You deserve it.

✳

We miss you and wish you a speedy recovery.
Nothing's the same when you're not here.

✳

Every day is a little better than the day before. Take it easy.

✳

Sending you wishes that each day brings you renewed strength
and a healthier and happier you.

✳

We are all wishing you happy healing and a speedy recovery.

Getting back to health is easy enough ... It's getting back to work
that's tough! Get well soon.

∗

Sending you heartfelt warmth and wishes,
hope you're feeling better soon.

∗

You are always doing so much for everyone else.
Please rest and let everyone wait on you.

∗

I was going to cook you some chicken soup ... then I thought,
wait (he/she) is sick already, leave the cooking to the experts.

∗

Looking forward to having you back on your feet ... it's not the same
without you. Get well soon.

∗

Won't be long and you will be your perky self again ...
enjoy the remote while you can.

∗

Life's no fun without you ... Get well soon.

∗

A kiss makes everything better ... here are two XX ... We miss you.
Get well soon.

∗

Ever feel like the universe is slowing you down?
Slow down and enjoy the pace and let others take care of you.

∗

Heard you were feeling a bit under the weather ...
hope the sun shines soon.

∗

Sending you a bouquet of healing wishes and a little ray of warm
sunshine.

Hang in there, you will be up on your feet and raring to go in no time.

✳

We have really missed having you around and seeing your sunny smile. Please get well soon... it's not the same without you.

✳

It was hard to see how badly this illness has knocked you about, but we are so glad to hear that you are on the mend.

✳

Make sure you milk it for all it's worth. Get well... but not too soon!

✳

Take your time; we have everything under control. We wish you a complete recovery and look forward to seeing you when you get back.

✳

I know you must be feeling pretty lousy, but make sure you take the time to enjoy daytime TV while you can. All our love.

✳

I always knew that you were indispensable. We will survive without you, but not for long. Hurry up and get well soon.

✳

Never again will I take all that you do for granted... especially in the kitchen. Please get well soon before we all die from food poisoning!

✳

Things are so quite and peaceful when you are not around stirring up trouble. Nonetheless we miss you dearly. Get well soon.

✳

If you are anything like me you will be wallowing in self-pity. It's fun isn't it?

✳

I heard you had the flu. Please let me know if there is anything I can do.

You are the most efficient and productive person I know. No doubt this means you will have a speedy and thorough recovery.

✻

You are always looking out for everyone else's needs. It's time to stop and let others take care of yours. Wishing you a steady and whole recovery. Best wishes.

✻

'Your body is like a bar of soap. It gradually wears down from repeated use.'
—Dick 'Richie' Allen (1942—), US baseball player

✻

'People who feel well are sick people neglecting themselves.'
—Jules Romains (1885—1972),
French novelist, playwright and poet

✻

The greatest healing therapy is friendship and love.
Hubert Humphrey

✻

The best six doctors anywhere
And no one can deny it
Are sunshine, water, rest, and air
Exercise and diet.
These six will gladly you attend
If only you are willing
Your mind they'll ease
Your will they'll mend
And charge you not a shilling.
Nursery rhyme quoted by Wayne Fields in *What the River Knows*

✻

Since you've been sick there's been a vacuum ... and no-one knows how to run it! Get Well Soon.   Unknown

✻

I wonder why you can always read a doctor's bill and you can never read his prescription.   Finley Peter Dunne

Sleep, riches, and health to be truly enjoyed must be interrupted.
Johann Paul Friedrich Richter

✳

There are many reasons for you to get well.
Your family loves and needs you,
your family is worried about you ...
... your family is totally unsupervised in your kitchen.
Unknown

✳

Get well cards have become so humorous that if you don't get sick
you're missing half the fun. Flip Wilson

✳

The treatment is really a cooperative of a trinity—the patient, the
doctor and the inner doctor. Ralph Bircher

✳

The best of healers is good cheer. Pindus

✳

There is no medicine like hope, no incentive so great, and no tonic
so powerful as expectation of something tomorrow. Orison Swett
Marden

✳

Sleep, riches and health to be truly enjoyed must be interrupted.
Johann Paul Friedrich Richter

✳

A bowl of warmth, a soft face, a new day. Some get-well thoughts
sent your way. Feel better soon. Unknown

✳

The art of medicine consists of amusing the patient while nature
cures the disease. Voltaire

✳

Your never know how much they care until you are under the
weather. C. Kohler

The greatest healing therapy is friendship and love. Hubert Humphrey

I enjoy convalescence. It is the part that makes the illness worth while. George Bernard Shaw

The best of healers is good cheer. Pindus

Be careful when reading health books; you may die of a misprint. Mark Twain

The power of love to change bodies is legendary, built into folklore, common sense, and everyday experience. Love moves the flesh, it pushes matter around... Throughout history, "tender loving care" has uniformly been recognized as a valuable element in healing. Larry Dossey

Pain is inevitable. Suffering is optional. M. Kathleen Casey

Sympathy

'Death is not the last sleep.
It is the final awakening.'
—Walter Scott (1771—1832),
Scottish novelist

We know there is so little we can do to help you bear the pain of loss
you are feeling, and so little we can say to help you through the day.
But may you know our deepest love and sympathy are with you.

✻

Although we don't always understand, God has a purpose for all things
and he will not let things overwhelm us beyond what we can bear.
Our love and prayers for strength are with you.

✻

We are so sorry to hear of the loss of your beloved [name].
We pray that soon you will be able to heal your heart
with fond memories of the times you shared.

✻

It is so hard to bear the loss of someone you love.
All our love and sympathy goes out to you.

✻

We are thinking of you at this time of loss and
extend to you our sympathy and understanding.

✻

With thoughts of deep sympathy on the loss of your [name].
As time goes by, may the memories of the good times you shared
never fade.

✻

During this time of sorrow, know that we are thinking of you,
and may you find peace in the memories you hold.

✻

We are so sorry to hear of your loss. Words don't seem to say enough.
But we hope, in some small way,
they may help to ease the pain you are feeling.

✻

There are no words to express the emptiness you must feel.
May fond memories be a comfort to you at this time
and may your heart soon be healed.

*

At this sad time no words can convey what we feel for you.
We pray that your pain and emptiness may soon ease and
that these few words will be a comfort to you.

*

At this sad and difficult time, our own hearts go out to you.
We are so very sorry to hear of your loss.

*

Saying goodbye to someone so close is the hardest thing to endure.
May you find comfort in the words and love of those close to you.

*

Losing a [name] is never easy. Please know we understand
your pain and are thinking of you during this difficult time.

*

Our deepest sympathy at your time of loss.
We pray your sorrow grows lighter as the days go by.

*

I know how difficult it is to say goodbye. I was so sorry to hear
of the loss of your beloved [name]. May memories of your
times together ease the ache in your heart.

*

Our deepest sympathy to you and your family at this time.
May fond memories bridge the gap between you and [name].

*

Words are not enough to express how sorry we were to hear of your
loss. May the precious memories you hold in your heart remain forever.

*

We were so sorry to hear of the loss of such a special person.
As the people who love you express their best wishes, may
you find comfort from the pain in your heart.

*

May [name] live forever through the memories of those close to him/
her. Our love and deepest sympathy to you and your family.
It is so hard to say good bye to a loved one. May you find
comfort in the loving thoughts of those around you.

*

Though we cannot fully share the pain you are feeling, you are always
in our thoughts and don't hesitate to call if there is anything you
need.

*

We take comfort in knowing [name of deceased] is no longer suffering.
[He/She] will remain in our hearts forever. We send thoughts of
comfort to you in your time of grieving.

*

[Name of deceased] was a blessing and a gift whose memory will be
cherished forever. Our hearts go out to you in your time of sorrow.

*

Please accept our condolences. We are thinking of you
at this difficult time.

*

Remembering you and your family at this difficult time.
Our sincerest sympathy.

*

Praying you find the strength you need to get through this profound
loss. [Name of deceased] will be sorely missed.

*

May the memories of your loved one never fade and be a constant
reminder of all that was beautiful in [Name's] time with you.

May you find comfort in knowing [name of deceased] touched the
lives of everyone they met and our lives have been enriched for
having known [him/her].

✳

May the memories of your time together bring you comfort.
[Name of deceased] will live on in all our hearts.

✳

Don't forget God is with you, by your side at this difficult time.
As are we, your friends and family.

✳

[Name of deceased] was a source of inspiration to many.
[He/She] will never be forgotten.

✳

May your heart find peace in the love of your
family and friends at this time.

✳

Please know I am here to help in any way. May your heart
and soul find peace and comfort during this difficult time.

✳

We will really miss [name] but we will never forget him/her. Thoughts
of admiration and love for [name] will always live on in our memories.

✳

[Name] was such a blessing to us all. It hurts so much to lose such a
wonderful person.

✳

I will always remember [name] when I am looking for inspiration. [He/
She] was such a great friend and mentor and will be dearly missed.

✳

Only God can fill the hole left by the loss of [name]. Look to Him and
let His love fill you and make you whole.

There are no words at this time. Just know that [we/I] am thinking of you and are so very sorry for your loss.

✳

Gone from our lives but not from our hearts or memories.

✳

May fond memories bring you peace and comfort.

✳

Don't struggle alone. Know that I am here to lean on to share your burden as you have always been here for me.

✳

I know this is a tough time for you right now and it is so hard to see you hurting, but know the sun will come out and warm your heart again.

✳

Never forget how much joy [name] gave to so many lives. May these fond thoughts bring you solace.

✳

Only time and happy memories will ease the pain that no words can.

✳

[Name] has left a legacy of love that will always be with you.

✳

There is never enough time with those we love. In time, happy memories will heal your broken heart.

✳

Remembering with you the life of [name], [he/she] will never be forgotten.

✳

[Name] will always be close in your memories and know that I will always be close if you need comfort.

'The way through the world is more difficult to find than the way beyond it.'
Wallace Stevens (1879–1955), US poet

*

'Earth hath no sorrow that heaven cannot heal.'
Thomas Moore (1478–1535), English statesman and author

*

'Better to light a candle than to curse the darkness.'
Chinese proverb

*

'To everything there is a season, and a time to every purpose under heaven.'
Ecclesiastes 3:1

*

'The journey is the reward.'
Chinese proverb

*

'It is love, not reason, that is stronger than death.'
Thomas Mann (1875–1955), German novelist

*

'Love comforteth, like sunshine after rain.'
William Shakespeare (1564–1616), *Venus and Adonis*

*

A human life is a story told by God.
Hans Christian Andersen

*

Unable are the loved to die. For love is immortality.
Emily Dickinson

*

When you are sorrowful look again in your heart, and you shall see that in truth you are weeping for that which has been your delight. Kahlil Gibran

In the night of death, hope sees a star, and listening love can hear the rustle of a wing. Robert Ingersoll

*

They that love beyond the world cannot be separated by it. Death cannot kill what never dies. William Penn

*

Although it's difficult today to see beyond the sorrow, May looking back in memory help comfort you tomorrow. Unknown

*

Death leaves a heartache no-one can heal, love leaves a memory no-one can steal. On a headstone

*

Perhaps they are not the stars, but rather openings in Heaven where the love of our lost ones pours through and shines down upon us to let us know they are happy. Unknown

*

Life is eternal, and love is immortal, and death is only a horizon; and a horizon is nothing save the limit of our sight. Rossiter Worthington Raymond

*

The most authentic thing about us is our capacity to create, to overcome, to endure, to transform, to love and to be greater than our suffering. Ben Okri

*

The season of mourning, like spring, summer, fall and winter, will also pass. Molly Fumia

*

While we are mourning the loss of our friend, others are rejoicing to meet him behind the veil. John Taylor

A human life is a story told by God. Hans Christian Andersen

To live in hearts we leave behind
Is not to die. Thomas Campbell, 'Hallowed Ground'

Oh heart, if one should say to you that the soul perishes like the body, answer that the flower withers, but the seed remains.
Kahlil Gibran

Retirement

Now you can take time to smell the flowers,
catch up on some sleep and enjoy the sunshine.

✳

It's not retirement—just a longer weekend.

✳

You have done your time and proved yourself to be one of the best.
We are going to miss you.

✳

It's all smooth sailing for you now—enjoy it.

✳

Downhill—with no load. Enjoy the ride.

✳

It's time to stop watching the clock.

✳

It's a wonderful time in your life. Congratulations and all the best.

✳

You have earned the right to take time to enjoy yourself.

✳

Best wishes for your new phase of life.

✳

Look forward to the days ahead—have a wonderful time.

✳

It's the time in your life to stop and see what's new.

✳

May you pursue your future dreams with ambition and determination.

✳

Enjoy those Monday morning sleep-ins.
Congratulations on your retirement.

The start of something new, you have earned it. Enjoy!

*

You have made such a difference in your time here.
You have touched and influenced so many. Thank you.

*

We will never forget all you have achieved.
Good luck in your retirement.

*

Look forward to each new day in happy anticipation ...
All the best for your retirement.

*

You have opened the door to a new beginning. Enjoy!

*

May this be the start of many new adventures. Congratulations.

*

You will be so missed. Please come and visit.

*

May good luck be with you in this new season of your life.

*

You were the key to our success.
Thank you and good luck in your new life.

*

I hope one day I will work again with someone as special as you.
All the best.

*

We will miss your expertise and wisdom. Good luck for the future.

*

May you have as much success in this new stage of life as you did in
your career. Congratulations on your retirement.

May you have as much creativity in your retirement as you did in the workplace.

✳

I hope when you think back on your time here with us you can't help but smile. I know I will when reminded of you in this place.

✳

Thank you for keeping this place shaken and stirred. It won't be the same without you.

✳

It has been such a privilege to have worked with you. I envy your new colleagues.

✳

I am going to miss seeing you around here. I hope your new co-workers appreciate you as much as we do.

✳

*'Working people have a lot of bad habits,
but the worst of these is work.'*
Clarence Darrow (1857–1938), US lawyer and debater

✳

*'Work is just another of man's diseases,
and prevention is better than cure.'*
Heathcote Williams (Born 1941), British playwright

✳

'It is time I stepped aside for a less experienced and less able man.'
US professor Scott Elledge (1914–1997),
on his retirement from Cornell University

✳

*Don't simply retire from something;
have something to retire to.   Harry Emerson Fosdick*

✳

*The challenge of retirement is how to spend time
without spending money.*   Unknown

When a man retires, his wife gets twice the husband but only half the income. Chi Chi Rodriguez

✳

When a man retires and time is no longer a matter of urgent importance, his colleagues generally present him with a watch. R C Sherriff

✳

When you retire, you switch bosses—from the one who hired you to the one who married you. Gene Perret

✳

The best time to start thinking about your retirement is before the boss does. Unknown

✳

A retired husband is often a wife's full-time job. Ella Harris

✳

Retirement is wonderful. It's doing nothing without worrying about getting caught at it. Gene Perret

✳

The trouble with retirement is that you never get a day off. Abe Lemons

✳

Retirement has been a discovery of beauty for me. I never had the time before to notice the beauty of my grandkids, my wife, the tree outside my very own front door. And, the beauty of time itself. Hartman Jule

✳

The question isn't at what age I want to retire, it's at what income. George Foreman

✳

When men reach their 60s and retire, they go to pieces. Women go right on cooking. Gail Sheehy

*I enjoy waking up and not having to go to work.
So I do it three or four times a day.* Gene Perret

✳

*Enjoy every retirement day as if it was your last and one day you
will be right about it.* Unknown

✳

*Retirement is wonderful if you have two essentials—much to live
on and much to live for.* Unknown

✳

I'm retired—goodbye tension, hello pension! Unknown

✳

*Retirement can be a great joy if you can figure out how to spend
time without spending money.* Unknown

✳

*Retired is being twice tired, I've thought
First tired of working,
Then tired of not.* Richard Armour

✳

*There is a whole new kind of life ahead, full of experiences just
waiting to happen. Some call it "retirement". I call it bliss.*
Betty Sullivan

✳

*I've been attending lots of seminars in my retirement. They're
called naps.* Merri Brownworth

✳

Retirement means doing whatever I want to do. It means choice.
Dianne Nahirny

Bon Voyage

'Until we meet again, may God hold you in the palm of his hand.'
—Irish blessing

May you prosper in everything you do and
wherever this journey takes you.

✳

We will miss your smiling face. Don't forget to
write or phone to let us know you are safe.

✳

Farewell on this new and exciting journey.

✳

Wherever you go, we know you will make an impression.

✳

We're going to miss you. Have a great trip and spare a thought
for us less fortunate.

✳

Wish I was coming too. Got room in your suitcase?

✳

Bon Voyage! Have an exciting and memorable holiday.

✳

May this holiday be the best one yet.

✳

Don't be gone too long ... we're going to miss you.
Have a great holiday.

✳

I hope you enjoy your time away and come back refreshed and full of
energy.

✳

While you're gone, spare a thought for us all slaving away and doing
your work as well. Have a great trip.

✳

'I won't soon forget you.'
—Shane Garrett, unknown

*'Love knows not its own depth until the hour of separation.
All farewells should be sudden.'*
Lord Byron (1788–1824), English poet

*

*'Parting is such sweet sorrow
That I shall say good night till it be morrow.'*
William Shakespeare (1564–1616), *Romeo and Juliet*

*

'You look after your half of the world, and I will look after mine.'
Shane Garrett, unknown

*

A vacation is having nothing to do and all day to do it in.
Robert Orben

*

*Remember—sometimes the road less travelled is less travelled
for a reason.* Jerry Seinfeld

*

*Those that say you can't take it with you never saw a car
packed for a vacation trip.* Unknown

*

A good vacation is over when you begin to yearn for your work.
Morris Fishbein

Travel and change of place impart new vigour to the mind. Seneca

*

*When preparing to travel, lay out all your clothes and all your
money. Then take half the clothes and twice the money.*
Susan Heller

*

*A sunbeam to warm you,
A moonbeam to charm you,
A sheltering angel,
so nothing can harm you.* Irish Blessing

Happy trails to you, until we meet again.
Some trails are happy ones,
Others are blue.
It's the way you ride the trail that counts,
Here's a happy one for you. Dale Evans

✳

To get away from one's working environment is, in a sense, to get
away from one's self; and this is often the chief advantage of
travel and change. Charles Horton Cooley

Apology

I am so sorry for what I have done. I will try to make it up
to you somehow. I hope our relationship is repairable.

✳

I will do anything to fix this mess I have made—
I am sorry for hurting you.

✳

I am so sorry for what I said and the way I have made you feel.
I didn't mean to hurt you.

✳

I hurt the one I love so much. I offer you my apology.
I am missing you so much—please forgive me.

✳

I am sorry for making you cry. I hurt because you hurt.
Can you ever forgive me?

Admitting I am wrong is a hard thing to do, but seeing you
hurt is the hardest of all. I'm sorry.

✳

I was wrong. Please forgive me. All I want more than anything
is your forgiveness and to kiss and make up.

✳

I'm so sorry for the hurt I have caused. I will have no peace
until you forgive me.

✳

Sorry I wasn't there for you when you needed someone to talk
to and a shoulder to cry on.

✳

Can you forgive me? I said words I did not mean, but know
I mean this ... I am sorry.

I'm sorry for what I've put you through. It must have been so hard for you. I wish I'd been a better friend. I hope this friendship we can mend.

✳

I know you are so understanding. It is your forgiving nature that makes me love you. Thank you for understanding.

✳

Please forgive me for the damage I have done. Just tell me what I need to do to make it up to you. Nothing would be too hard or too much for your love and forgiveness.

✳

I am so sorry. I hope it is not too late.
Please tell me we are not beyond repair.

✳

I was wrong, you were right ... Sorry.

✳

An apology is a good way to have the last word.
Unknown

✳

I can't forgive myself but I hope you can... Sorry.

✳

I would do anything to be able to turn back the hands of time. Please forgive me.

✳

I made a big boo boo. Please forgive me.

✳

I am sorry for the mistakes I have made. I am sending a big hug to you so that you might know how much I love you.

✳

I did not mean to upset you. I am sorry for the insensitive things I said.

Once again I have put my foot in it. I am sorry.

✱

I am finding it hard to forgive myself it must be a million times harder for you. I am sorry.

✱

I am wrong... You are right.

✱

I was foolish, I did not think. Please grant me your forgiveness.

✱

There is no excuse for the way I behaved. I am beyond sorry. Please forgive me.

✱

OOPS... my mistake, sorry.

✱

Please accept this [gift/flowers] as a small token of how sorry I am. It will never happen again.

✱

I am so embarrassed to have to make this apology but even more embarrassed by what I have done. Please forgive me, it will never happen again.

✱

I appreciate the patience you have shown me, but even more I appreciate your forgiveness and unconditional love.

✱

I know I cannot undo the damage I have done, but please know it was never my intention to hurt you. I am sincerely sorry.

✱

*In some families, 'please' is described as the magic word.
In our house, however, it was 'sorry'.* Margaret Laurence

Apology is a lovely perfume; it can transform the clumsiest moment into a gracious gift. Margaret Lee Runbeck

✳

For every minute you are angry, you lose sixty seconds of happiness. Unknown

✳

Keep your words soft and tender because tomorrow you may have to eat them. Unknown

✳

Never ruin an apology with an excuse. Kimberly Johnson

✳

Never apologise for showing feeling. When you do so, you apologise for the truth. Benjamin Disraeli

✳

An apology is the super glue of life. It can repair just about anything. Lynn Johnston

✳

Forgiveness does not change the past, but it does enlarge the future. Paul Boese

✳

An apology is a good way to have the last word. Unknown

✳

It is easier to forgive an enemy than to forgive a friend. William Blake

✳

Right actions in the future are the best apologies for bad actions in the past. Tryon Edwards

✳

The most important trip you may take in life is meeting people halfway. Henry Boye

Not the fastest horse can catch a word spoken in anger.
Chinese Proverb

The only correct actions are those that demand no explanation and no apology. Red Auerbach

Business

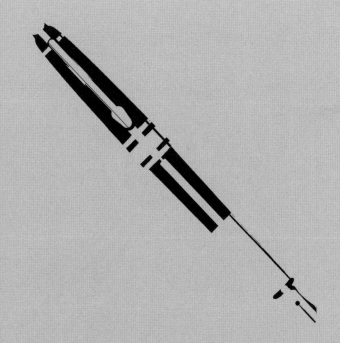

'What's worth doing is worth doing for money.'
Joseph Donahue, quoted in *The Official Rule*

✻

'Money is the sixth sense that makes it possible
to enjoy the other five.'
Richard Ney (1915–2004),
US actor, writer and investment adviser

✻

'A billion here, a billion there, and soon
you're talking about real money.'
Everett Dirksen (1896–1969) US senator

✻

'If you can count your money, you don't have a billion dollars.'
J Paul Getty (1892–1976) US oil industrialist

✻

'If you don't drive your business you will be driven out of business.'
BC Forbes (1880–1954) US publisher

✻

'I am opposed to millionaires, but it would be dangerous to offer
me the position.'
Mark Twain (1835–1910), American author and humorist

✻

'A large income is the best recipe for happiness I ever heard of.'
Jane Austen (1775–1817), *Northanger Abbey*

Inspirational Quotes

When you cease to dream, you cease to live. Malcolm Forbes

✻

If you don't go after what you want, you'll never have it. If you don't ask, the answer is always 'no'. If you don't step forward, you're always in the same place. Nora Roberts

✻

The ultimate measure of a man is not where he stands in moments of comfort and convenience, but where he stands at times of challenge and controversy. Martin Luther King, Jr

✻

One can never consent to creep when one feels an impulse to soar. Helen Keller

✻

We cannot direct the wind but we can adjust the sails. Unknown

✻

The future belongs to those who believe in the beauty of their dreams. Eleanor Roosevelt

✻

When you were born, you cried and the world rejoiced. Live your life so that when you die, the world cries and you rejoice. Cherokee saying

✻

Faith is taking the first step even when you don't see the whole staircase. Martin Luther King, Jr

✻

Look at a day when you are supremely satisfied at the end. It's not a day when you lounge around doing nothing; it's when you've had everything to do, and you've done it. Lord Acton

✻

Our greatest GLORY is not in never failing ... but in RISING every time we fall. Confucius

Do not go where the path may lead, go instead where there is no path and leave a trail.   Ralph Waldo Emerson

✳

Only he who can see the invisible can do the impossible.
Frank L Gaines

✳

Only those who will risk going too far can possibly find out how far one can go.   T S Eliot

✳

Begin with the end in mind.   Stephen Covey

✳

Shoot for the moon. Even if you miss, you'll land among the stars.
Les Brown

✳

Most of the important things in the world have been accomplished by people who have kept on trying when there seemed to be no hope at all.   Dale Carnegie

✳

To accomplish great things, we must not only act, but also dream; not only plan, but also believe. Anatole France

✳

Every artist was first an amateur. Ralph Waldo Emerson

✳

Men's best successes come after their disappointments.
Henry Ward Beecher

✳

Every day, do something that will inch you closer to a better tomorrow. Doug Firebaugh

✳

Don't count the days, make the days count. Muhammad Ali

The best way to make your dreams come true is to wake up!
Paul Valery

First say to yourself what you would be;
and then do what you have to do. Epictetus

To find what you seek in the road of life,
the best proverb of all is that which says:
"Leave no stone unturned." Edward Bulwer Lytton

Happiness Quotes

Happiness is not a state to arrive at, but a manner of travelling.
Margaret Lee Runbeck

✻

The grand essentials of happiness are: something to do, something to love, and something to hope for. Allan K Chalmers

✻

Nobody really cares if you're miserable, so you might as well be happy. Cynthia Nelms

✻

The happiest moments of my life have been the few which I have passed at home in the bosom of my family. Thomas Jefferson

✻

The foolish man seeks happiness in the distance, the wise grows it under his feet. James Oppenheim

✻

Happiness is never stopping to think if you are. Palmer Sondreal

✻

You need to learn to be happy by nature, because you'll seldom have the chance to be happy by circumstance.
Lavetta Sue Wegman

✻

Love is a condition in which the happiness of another person is essential to your own. Robert Heinlein

✻

Happiness is when what you think, what you say, and what you do are in harmony. Mohandas K Gandhi

✻

Whoever is happy will make others happy, too. Mark Twain

Success is not the key to happiness. Happiness is the key to success. If you love what you are doing, you will be successful.
Albert Schweitzer

✳

Happiness is having a large, loving, caring, close-knit family in another city. George Burns

✳

Wherever you go, no matter what the weather, always bring your own sunshine. Anthony J D'Angelo

✳

When one door of happiness closes, another opens; but often we look so long at the closed door that we do not see the one which has been opened for us. Helen Keller

✳

Happiness is nothing more than good health and a bad memory.
Albert Schweitzer

✳

Happiness is as a butterfly which, when pursued,
is always beyond our grasp,
but which if you will sit down quietly, may alight upon you.
Nathaniel Hawthorne

✳

Let us be grateful to people who make us happy; they are the charming gardeners who make our souls blossom. Marcel Proust

✳

One of the keys to happiness is a bad memory. Rita Mae Brown

✳

Knowledge of what is possible is the beginning of happiness.
George Santayana

✳

Most people are about as happy as they make up their minds to be. Abraham Lincoln

If you want to be happy, set a goal that commands your thoughts, liberates your energy and inspires your hopes. Andrew Carnegie

✳

Happiness is not a matter of events, it depends upon the tides of the mind. Alice Meynell

✳

There is only one person who could ever make you happy, and that person is you. David Burns, *Intimate Connections*

✳

You're happiest while you're making the greatest contribution. Robert F. Kennedy

✳

Happiness resides not in possessions and not in gold; the feeling of happiness dwells in the soul. Democritus

✳

The amount of happiness that you have depends on the amount of freedom you have in your heart. Unknown

✳

Happiness depends more on the inward disposition of mind than on outward circumstances. Benjamin Franklin

✳

People with many interests live, not only longest, but happiest. George Matthew Allen

✳

Happiness is a perfume you cannot pour on others without getting a few drops on yourself. Unknown

✳

Who is the happiest of men? He who values the merits of others, and in their pleasure takes joy, even as though 'twere his own. Johann Wolfgang von Goethe

Love Quotes

'To live without loving is to not really live.'
Molière (1622–73), French comic playwright

✳

*'Love consists in this, that two solitudes protect and touch
and greet each other.'*
Rainer Maria Rilke (1875–1926), German poet and author

✳

'We are shaped and fashioned by what we love.'
Johann Wolfgang von Goethe (1749–1842), German author

✳

*'Take Spring when it comes and rejoice. Take happiness when it
comes and rejoice. Take love when it comes and rejoice.'*
Carl Ewald (1856–1908), Danish writer

✳

*'And think not you can guide the course of love.
For love, if it finds you worthy, shall guide your course.'*
Kahlil Gibran (1883–1931),
Lebanese–US poet, philosopher and artist

✳

*'One man by himself is nothing. Two people who
belong together make a world.'*
Hans Margolius (1902–) German philosopher

✳

*'No love, no friendship, can cross the path of our destiny
without leaving some mark on it forever.'*
Francois Mauriac (1885–1970),
French novelist and Nobel laureate

✳

*'Love does not consist in gazing at each other,
but in looking together in the same direction.'*
Antoine de Saint-Exupéry (1900–44), French pilot and poet

'The quarrels of lovers are like summer storms.
Everything is more beautiful when they have passed.'
Suzanne Necker (1773–1794), French writer

✳

'There is no remedy for love but to love more.'
Henry David Thoreau (1817–1862)
US author, poet and philosopher

✳

'He who love touches walks not in darkness.'
Plato (427–347 BC), Greek philosopher

✳

'The entire sum of existence is the magic of
being needed by just one person.'
Vii Putnam, US writer

✳

'They gave each other a smile with a future in it.'
Ring Lardner (1885–1933), US writer

✳

'Gather the rose of love whilst yet is time.'
Edmund Spenser (1552–1599), English writer and poet

✳

'Treasure each other in the recognition that
we do not know how long we shall have each other.'
Joshua Liebman (1907–1948) US writer

✳

'Perhaps love is the process of my gently leading you back to
yourself.'
Antoine de Saint-Exupéry (1900–44), French pilot and poet

✳

'Love is the only gold.'
Alfred Lord Tennyson (1809–1892) English poet

'Love is the greatest refreshment in life.'
Pablo Picasso (1881–1973), Spanish painter

✳

'At the touch of love, everyone becomes a poet.'
Plato (427–347 BC), Greek philosopher

✳

'Love is perhaps the only glimpse we are permitted of eternity.'
Helen Hayes (1900–1993), US actor

✳

'To love and be loved is the greatest happiness of existence.'
Sydney Smith (1771–1845), English clergyman and essayist

✳

*'I beseech you now with all my heart definitely to let me
know your whole mind as to the love between us.'*
William Shakespeare (1564–1616), *King Henry VIII*

✳

'To love someone is to see a miracle invisible to others.'
Francois Mauriac (1885–1970),
French novelist and Nobel laureate

✳

*'If you press me to say why I loved him, I can say
no more than it was because he was he and I was I.'*
Michel de Montaigne (1553–1592), French essayist

✳

*'The last of your kisses was ever the sweetest; the last smile
the brightest; the last movement the gracefullest.'*
John Keats (1795–1821), English poet

✳

*'I have spread my dreams beneath your feet;
Tread softly because you tread on my dreams.'*
W.B. Yeats (1865–1939) Irish poet, essayist and
Nobel laureate

✳

Anyone can catch your eye, but it takes someone special to catch your heart. Unknown

✳

Love is like playing the piano. First you must learn to play by the rules, then you must forget the rules and play from your heart. Unknown

✳

To truly love someone is to put their feelings entirely before your own. Anne Marie Cline

✳

All love that has not friendship for its base, is like a mansion built upon the sand. Ella Wheeler Wilcox

✳

I've fallen in love many times ... always with you. Unknown

✳

True loves comes quietly, without banners or flashing lights. If you hear bells, get your ears checked. Erich Segal

✳

If love is blind, why is lingerie so popular? Unknown

✳

A kiss is a lovely trick designed by nature to stop speech when words become superfluous. Ingrid Bergman

✳

*I love you like crazy, baby.
'Cuz I'd go crazy without you.* Pixie Foudre

✳

Time is too slow for those who wait, too swift for those who fear, too long for those who grieve, too short for those who rejoice, but for those who love, time is eternity. Henry Van Dyke

✳

Love is like a violin. The music may stop now and then, but the strings remain forever. Unknown

✳

We love because it's the only true adventure. Nikki Giovanni

✳

Grow old with me! The best is yet to be. Robert Browning

✳

The most important things are the hardest to say, because words diminish them. Stephen King

✳

Are we not like two volumes of one book?
Marceline Desbordes-Valmore

✳

Love is missing someone whenever you're apart, but somehow feeling warm inside because you're close in heart. Kay Knudsen

✳

Anyone can be passionate, but it takes real lovers to be silly.
Rose Franken

✳

Life is the flower for which love is the honey. Victor Hugo

✳

Love doesn't make the world go round, love is what makes the ride worthwhile. Elizabeth Barrett Browning

✳

Love builds bridges where there are none. R H Delaney

✳

Love is a game that two can play and both win. Eva Gabor

✳

I love thee to the depth and breadth and height my soul can reach.
Elizabeth Barrett Browning

Attention is the most basic form of love; through it we bless and are blessed. John Tarrant

✳

Love is the master key that opens the gates of happiness. Oliver Wendell Holmes

✳

Love is the irresistible desire to be irresistibly desired. Mark Twain

✳

I love thee — I love thee,
'Tis all that I can say
It is my vision in the night,
My dreaming in the day.
Thomas Hood

Who, being loved, is poor? Oscar Wilde

✳

Love would never be a promise of a rose garden unless it is showered with light of faith, water of sincerity and air of passion. Unknown

✳

Love makes your soul crawl out from its hiding place. Zora Neale Hurston

✳

The heart that loves is always young. Unknown

✳

Love is like dew that falls on both nettles and lilies. Swedish proverb

✳

Love is the enchanted dawn of every heart. Lamartine

✳

We are all a little weird and life's a little weird, and when we find someone whose weirdness is compatible with ours, we join up with them and fall in mutual weirdness and call it love. Unknown

✳

True love stories never have endings. Richard Bach

✳

Love is the poetry of the senses. Honoré de Balzac

✳

Love puts the fun in together, the sad in apart, and the joy in a heart. Unknown

✳

Love is like an hourglass, with the heart filling up as the brain empties. Jules Renard

✳

Love unlocks doors and opens windows that weren't even there before. Mignon McLaughlin

✳

Love will find a way through paths where wolves fear to prey. Lord Byron

✳

The greatest science in the world, in heaven and on earth, is love. Mother Teresa

✳

There is more hunger for love and appreciation in this world than for bread. Mother Teresa

✳

I love her and that's the beginning of everything. F. Scott Fitzgerald

✳

A loving relationship is one in which the loved one is free to be himself—to laugh with me, but never at me; to cry with me, but never because of me; to love life, to love himself, to love being loved. Such a relationship is based upon freedom and can never grow in a jealous heart. Leo F. Buscaglia

✳

Keep love in your heart. A life without it is like a sunless garden when the flowers are dead. The consciousness of loving and being loved brings a warmth and a richness to life that nothing else can bring. Oscar Wilde

The Eskimos had fifty-two names for snow because it was important to them: there ought to be as many for love. Margaret Atwood

✳

Love is like a beautiful flower which I may not touch, but whose fragrance makes the garden a place of delight just the same. Helen Keller

✳

If you judge people, you have no time to love them. Mother Teresa

✳

I have learned not to worry about love;
But to honour its coming with all my heart. Alice Walker

✳

In the arithmetic of love, one plus one equals everything, and two minus one equals nothing. Mignon McLaughlin

✳

Being deeply loved by someone gives you strength; loving someone deeply gives you courage. Lao Tzu

✳

A smile is the lighting system of the face, the cooling system of the head and the heating system of the heart. Unknown

Love comforteth like sunshine after rain.
William Shakespeare

✳

I've learned that people will forget what you said, people will forget what you did, but people will never forget how you made them feel. Maya Angelou

✳

Above all things I believe in love. Love is like oxygen. Love is a many-splendoured thing. Love lifts us up where we belong. All you need is love!
From the movie *Moulin Rouge* (2001)

✳

All, everything that I understand, I understand only because I love.
Leo Tolstoy

✳

Love is that condition in which the happiness of another person is essential to your own. Robert A. Heinlein

✳

Love is a path to the heart that knows its own way. Lamar Cole

✳

Believe in the importance of love, for it is the strength and beauty that brings music to our souls. Unknown

✳

Dance as though no one is watching you. Love as though you have never been hurt before. Sing as though no one can hear you. Live as though heaven is on earth. Unknown

✳

Do you want me to tell you something really subversive? Love is everything it's cracked up to be. That's why people are so cynical about it... It really is worth fighting for, being brave for, risking everything for. And the trouble is, if you don't risk anything, you risk even more. Erica Jong

✳

I'm not supposed to love you, I'm not supposed to care, I'm not supposed to live my life wishing you were there. I'm not supposed to wonder where you are or what you do... I'm sorry I can't help myself, I'm in love with you. Unknown

✳

Don't frown because you never know who might be falling in love with your smile. Unknown

✳

Love has nothing to do with what you are expecting to get—only with what you are expecting to give—which is everything. Katharine Hepburn

Life without love is like a tree without blossoms or fruit. Kahlil Gibran

✳

In true love the smallest distance is too great, and the greatest distance can be bridged. Hans Nouwens

✳

Love is like fever; it comes and goes without the will having any part in the process. Henry Beyle Stendahl

✳

Love is taking a few steps backwards (maybe even more)... to give way to the happiness of the person you love. Unknown

✳

Love demands all and has a right to it. Beethoven

✳

Falling in love with someone isn't always going to be easy... anger... tears... laughter... It's when you want to be together despite it all. That's when you truly love another. I'm sure of it. Unknown

✳

For all that you are and all that you do, and for the many ways you make my heart sing. Leland Thomas

*If I could give you one gift, I would give you the ability to see
yourself as I see you, so you could see how truly special you are.*
Unknown

✳

*Once in awhile, right in the middle of an ordinary life, love gives us
a fairy tale.* Unknown

✳

A life without love is like a year without summer.
Swedish proverb

✳

*I am so glad that you are here... It helps me realise how beautiful
my world is.* Johann Wolfgang von Goethe

✳

*Goodnight! Goodnight!
Parting is such sweet sorrow
That I shall say goodnight 'til it be morrow.*
William Shakespeare

Bible Love Quotes

*'A new commandment I give unto you, that ye love one another;
as I have loved you, that ye also love one another.'*
John 13:34

✳

*'Love never faileth; but where there be prophecies, they shall fail;
where there be tongues, they shall cease, where there be
knowledge, it shall vanish away.'*
1 Corinthians 13

✳

'There is no fear in love; but perfect love casteth out fear.'
1 John 4:18

Funny Quotes

*'Some mornings it just doesn't seem worth it
to gnaw through the leather straps.'*
Emo Phillips, US comedian

✳

*'I try to take one day at a time, but sometimes
several days attack me at once.'*
Ashleigh Brilliant (1933–), US humorist and cartoonist

✳

*'The Bible tells us to love our neighbours, and also to love our
enemies; probably because generally they are the same people.'*
Gilbert Chesterton (1874–1936), English essayist,
critic and author

✳

*'Only presidents, editors, and people with tapeworms
have the right to use the editorial "we".'*
Mark Twain (1835–1910), US author and humorist

✳

*'By all means marry. If you get a good wife, you'll be happy.
If you get a bad one, you'll become a philosopher*
Socrates (469–399 BC), Athenian philosopher

✳

*'There are terrible temptations which it requires
strength and courage to yield to.'*
Oscar Wilde (1854–1900), Irish dramatist and novelist

✳

*'Anyone who can only think of only one way
to spell a word obviously lacks imagination.'*
Mark Twain (1835–1910), US author and humorist

✳

'Everything is funny as long as it is happening to somebody else.'
Will Rogers (1879–1935), US actor and humorist

'All modern men are descended from worm-like creatures,
but it shows more on some people.'
Will Cuppy (1884–1949), US humorist and journalist

✻

'The most important service rendered by the press is that of
educating people to approach printed matter with distrust.'
Samuel Butler (1612–1680) English poet and satirist

✻

'The only way of catching a train I ever discovered
is to miss the train before.'
Gilbert Chesterton (1874–1936) English essayist,
critic and author

✻

'Bad spellers of the world—Untie!'
Graffiti

✻

'Always do right. That will gratify some of the people,
and astonish the rest.'
Mark Twain (1835–1910), US author and humorist

✻

'Three may keep a secret if two of them are dead.'
Benjamin Franklin (1706–90), US statesman, diplomat, author,
scientist and inventor

✻

'It is impossible to enjoy idling thoroughly
unless one has plenty of work to do.'
Jerome K. Jerome (1859–1927) English humorist, novelist and
playwright

✻

'Hanging is too good for a man who makes puns; he should be
drawn and quoted.'
Fred Allen (1894–1956), US comedian

'Anyone who is considered funny will tell you, sometimes without even your asking, that deep inside they are very serious, neurotic, introspective people.'
Wendy Wasserstein (1950–), US playwright

✳

'It is better to keep your mouth shut and appear stupid than to open it and remove all doubt.'
Mark Twain (1835–1910), US author and humorist

✳

'If I owned both Texas and Hell, I'd rent out Texas and live in Hell.'
Philip Henry Sheridan (1831–1888), US general

✳

'The reasonable man adapts himself to the world; the unreasonable man persists in trying to adapt the world to himself. Therefore, all progress depends on the unreasonable man.'
George Bernard Shaw (1856–1950), Irish dramatist, critic and novelist

✳

'The power of accurate observation is commonly called cynicism by those who have not got it.'
George Bernard Shaw (1856–1950), Irish dramatist, critic and novelist

✳

'A man may be a fool and not know it, but not if he is married.'
H.L. Mencken (1880–1935), US journalist and critic

✳

'What is the difference between a taxidermist and a tax collector? The taxidermist takes only your skin.'
Mark Twain (1835–1910), US author and humorist

✳

To let a fool kiss you is bad ... to let a kiss fool you is worse.
Unknown

✳

Kids in the back seat cause accidents. Accidents in the back seat cause ... kids. Unknown

Adults are always asking little kids what they want to be when they grow up because they're looking for ideas. Paula Poundstone

✳

Take my advice. I'm not using it. Unknown

✳

If you expect breakfast in bed, go sleep in the kitchen. Unknown

✳

Mirror, mirror on the wall, I've become my mother after all!
Unknown

✳

An archeologist is the best husband any woman can have; the older she gets, the more interested he is in her. Agatha Christie

✳

You can't put a price tag on love, but you can on all its accessories. Melanie Clark

✳

The Japanese have a word for it. It's Judo — the art of conquering by yielding. The Western equivalent of judo is, 'Yes, dear'.
J P McEvoy

✳

What I'm looking for is a blessing that's not in disguise.
Kitty O'Neill Collins

✳

Few things are more satisfying than seeing your children have teenagers of their own. Doug Larson

✳

Use your health, even to the point of wearing it out.
George Bernard Shaw

✳

When I'm finally holding all the cards, why does everyone decide to play chess? Unknown

✳

Girls are like phones. We love to be held and talked to but if you press the wrong button you'll be disconnected! Unknown

✳

The only time the world beats a path to your door is when you're in the bathroom. Unknown

✳

I want my children to have all the things I couldn't afford. Then I want to move in with them. Phyllis Diller

✳

Thank you. We're all refreshed and challenged by your unique point of view. Unknown

✳

I love to give homemade gifts... umm, which one of the kids would you like? Unknown

✳

You can observe a lot just by watching. Yogi Berra

✳

The fact that no one understands you doesn't mean you're an artist. Unknown

✳

If you're not living life on the edge you're taking up too much space. Unknown

✳

I like you. You remind me of when I was young and stupid.
Unknown

✳

If at first you don't succeed, then skydiving definitely isn't for you.
Unknown

✳

I will always cherish the initial misconceptions I had about you.
Unknown

✻

The man who smiles when things go wrong has thought of someone to blame it on. Robert Bloch

✻

Blessed is the person who is too busy to worry in the daytime and too sleepy to worry at night. Unknown

✻

God bless you and grant you twice what you wish me! Unknown

✻

How can a woman be expected to be happy with a man who insists on treating her as if she were a perfectly normal human being. Oscar Wilde

✻

I don't repeat gossip, so listen closely the first time! Unknown

✻

I've got what it takes, but nobody wants it. Unknown

✻

The spiritual eyesight improves as the physical eyesight declines.
Plato

✻

Lead me not into temptation; I can find it myself. Unknown

✻

If love is blind, why is lingerie so popular? Unknown

✻

If we are what we eat, then I'm fast, cheap and easy. Unknown
✻
When you meet someone who can cook and do housework—don't hesitate a minute—marry him. Unknown

Although the tongue weighs very little, few people are able to hold it. Unknown

✳

The average woman would rather have beauty than brains, because the average man can see better than he can think. Unknown

✳

Children are like mosquitoes: the minute they stop making noise, they're into something. Unknown

Cute Quotes

'If you can't be a good example, then you'll just have to be a horrible warning.'
Catherine Aird (1930–), English author

✻

'Nothing is so useless as a general maxim.'
Lord Macaulay (1800–1859), English essayist, historian, poet and politician

✻

'Education, like neurosis, begins at home.'
Milton R. Sapirstein (died 1996), US psychologist and author

✻

'I could see that, if not actually disgruntled, he was far from being gruntled.'
Pelham Grenville Wodehouse (1881–1975), English novelist

✻

'The brain is a wonderful organ; it starts working the moment you get up in the morning, and does not stop until you get into the office.'
Robert Frost (1874–1963), US poet

✻

'Do not take life too seriously; you will never get out of it alive.'
Elbert Hubbard (1856–1915), US author and publisher

✻

'Never keep up with the Joneses. Drag them down to your level. It's cheaper.'
Quentin Crisp (1908–1999), English writer

✻

'Man has made use of his intelligence; he invented stupidity.'
Remy de Gourmont (1858–1915), French critic and novelist

✻

'When people agree with me I always feel I must be wrong.'
Oscar Wilde (1854–1900), Irish dramatist and novelist

'The world is full of willing people; some willing to work,
the rest willing to let them.'
Robert Frost (1874–1963), US poet

*

'It's a dog-eat-dog world, and I'm wearing milk bone underwear.'
Norm, from the TV show *Cheers*

*

'It's not whether you win or lose, but how you place the blame.'
Anonymous

*

'It is inexcusable for scientists to torture animals; let them
make their experiments on journalists and politicians.'
Henrik Ibsen (1828–1906), Norwegian playwright and poet

*

'Many of us spend half our time wishing for things
we could have if we didn't spend half our time wishing.'
Alexander Woollcott (1887–1943), US author and journalist

Goodbye/Farewell

We're going to miss you. Please don't be a stranger
and visit once in a while.

*

Sorry to see you leaving. It has been a pleasure having you around.

*

Goodbye and Good Luck.

*

Things won't be the same when you're gone. We'll miss you.

*

You made coming to work more enjoyable. You'll be missed.

*

Take me with you.

*

I don't like goodbyes, so I'll just say 'Till we meet again'.

*

Sorry you are leaving but I am honoured to have known you.
All the best with wherever life takes you.

*

One of the highlights of my life has been knowing you.
I know this is not the end.

*

May this new path your life is taking lead you to wonderful places.

*

We are ending this chapter of our lives together but the book is not
over. I will miss you so much and I know we will see each other again.

*

It's not goodbye it's badbye. I can't believe you're leaving me.

*

I refuse to say goodbye... there is nothing good about you leaving.

Even though you will be miles away, you will still be in my thoughts. Let's not let the distance spoil our friendship.

✳

You are such a special person and your destiny is to go far and achieve much. I hope the people at your new work/in your new neighbourhood appreciate just how special you are.

✳

Why can't we get together all the people we really like and never have anyone leave? I will miss you more than you will ever know.

✳

Don't be dismayed at goodbyes. A farewell is necessary before you can meet again. And meeting again, after moments or a lifetime, is certain for those who are friends. Richard Bach

✳

Don't cry because it's over. Smile because it happened.
Attributed to Theodor Seuss Geisel

✳

Man's feelings are always purest and most glowing in the hour of meeting and of farewell. Jean Paul Richter

✳

Goodbye to someone we'll always remember ... from the weird bunch you probably can't wait to forget. Unknown

✳

Those to whom we say farewell, are welcomed by others.
Unknown

✳

The return makes one love the farewell. Alfred De Musset

✳

Why does it take a minute to say hello and forever to say goodbye? Unknown

No distance of place or lapse of time can lessen the friendship of those who are thoroughly persuaded of each other's worth.
Robert Southey

✳

A goodbye isn't painful unless you're never going to say hello again. Unknown

✳

A man never knows how to say goodbye; a woman never knows when to say it. Helen Rowland

✳

May the road rise up to meet you, may the wind be ever at your back. May the sun shine warm upon your face and the rain fall softly on your fields. And until we meet again, may God hold you in the hollow of his hand. Irish Blessing

✳

Absence diminishes little passions and increases great ones, as the wind extinguishes candles and fans a fire.
Francois Duc de la Rochefoucauld, translated from French

✳

Only in the agony of parting do we look into the depths of love.
George Eliot

✳

Can miles truly separate you from friends... If you want to be with someone you love, aren't you already there? Richard Bach

✳

The world is a book, and those who do not travel read only a page. St. Augustine

✳

You and I will meet again,
When we're least expecting it,
One day in some far off place,
I will recognise your face,
I won't say goodbye my friend,
For you and I will meet again. Tom Petty

Nothing makes the earth seem so spacious as to have friends at a distance; they make the latitudes and longitudes. Henry David Thoreau

We only part to meet again. John Gay

UK £7.99